Interactive Student Centered Learning

Interactive Student Centered Learning

A Cooperative Approach to Learning

Edward Spooner

ROWMAN & LITTLEFIELD
Lanham • Boulder • New York • London

Published by Rowman & Littlefield
A wholly owned subsidiary of The Rowman & Littlefield Publishing Group, Inc.
4501 Forbes Boulevard, Suite 200, Lanham, Maryland 20706
www.rowman.com

Unit A, Whitacre Mews, 26-34 Stannery Street, London SE11 4AB

Copyright © 2015 by Edward Spooner

All rights reserved. No part of this book may be reproduced in any form or by any electronic or mechanical means, including information storage and retrieval systems, without written permission from the publisher, except by a reviewer who may quote passages in a review.

British Library Cataloguing in Publication Information Available

Library of Congress Cataloging-in-Publication Data

Library of Congress Cataloging-in-Publication Data Available
ISBN 978-1-4758-1347-0 (cloth : alk. paper) -- ISBN 978-1-4758-1348-7 (pbk. : alk. paper) -- ISBN 978-1-4758-1349-4 (electronic)

∞™ The paper used in this publication meets the minimum requirements of American National Standard for Information Sciences Permanence of Paper for Printed Library Materials, ANSI/NISO Z39.48-1992.

Printed in the United States of America

Contents

Preface: A Word from the Author	ix
Introduction	xi
1 The Learning Process	1
Educational Learning Theories	1
Learning Theories	6
Evolving Theories of Learning	8
Factors that Affect Learning	11
The Art of Teaching and Learning	12
Key Ideas to Remember	14
2 Traditional Learning/Teaching	17
The Objectives of TCL	19
Learning versus Student-Centered Learning	23
Key Ideas to Remember	24
3 Active Learning	25
Definitions	27
The Process	29
Problems	34
4 Cooperative Learning	37
Types of Cooperative Learning	41
Benefits of Cooperative Learning	42
Cooperative Learning Limitations	45
Why Does Cooperative Learning Work?	46
The Instructor's Role	46
Group/Team Process	47
Key Ideas to Remember	49

Contents

5	**Collaborative Learning**	51
	Research	52
	The Process	53
	Learning Objectives	54
	Benefits of Collaborative Learning	55
	Collaborative Handicaps	56
	Preparing Students for Group Work	57
	Key Ideas to Remember	63
6	**Constructivist Learning Theory**	65
	How Students Learn in a Constructive Environment	67
	The Nature of the Learner	68
	The Benefits of Constructivism	68
	Criticism of Educational Constructivism	69
	Instructors as a Facilitator	69
	Key Ideas to Remember	72
7	**Student Centered Learning**	73
	The Basic Concepts	73
	Teacher's Role as a Facilitator	76
	Assessment	78
	Benefits	80
	Disadvantages	82
	Group/Teamwork	83
8	**Interactive Student Centered Learning (1)**	87
	The Process	87
	Learning Objectives	89
	The Instructor's Role	90
	Assessment-Evaluation	93
	Student Group Participation	95
	Key Ideas to Remember	97
9	**Interactive Student Centered Learning (2)**	99
	Instructional Development	99
	Instructional Management	101
	Instructional Strategies	102
	Handbook	103
	Team/Group Participation	105
	Key Ideas to Remember	107
10	**Interactive Student Centered Learning (3)**	109
	Program Development	109
	Keys to Remember	112
	Appendix A: Student Handbook	115
	Instructor's Information	115

Letter to Students	115
Course Description	117
Purpose of Course	118
Class Responsibilities Guideline	119
Curriculum Objectives	119
How to Study for This Course	120
Self-Management	121
Student Responsibilities Contract	121
Sample of Student Contract	122
Learning Contract	124
Learning Style Inventory	125
Study Skills	125
Communication: The Key to Learning	126
Reading to Learn	128
Appendix B: Department of Physical Education and Health	**131**
How to Use This Syllabus	131
Class Organization and Structure	132
Tentative Course Calendar	133
Course Requirements	134
Goal Development	136
Goal Establishment	138
The P's and D's—Keys to Achieving Goal Success	139
Appendix C: Student Workbook: Class Organization and Structure	**141**
Student Activities and Daily Schedules	141
Panel/Debate Guidelines	146
Key Points to Remember	155
Appendix D: Additional Information	**157**
The Learning Process	157
Key Ideas to Remember	170
References	**173**
Active Learning	173
Cooperative Learning	173
Collaborative Learning	174
Constructivism Learning	174
Student-Centered Learning	174
About the Author	**175**

Preface

A Word from the Author

After critically examining the major elements of each learning/teaching method frequently discussed in the literature, I found that research in neuroscience, biology and cognitive psychology, and various teaching philosophies indicate that student centered learning/teaching (SCL) is relevant at almost all levels of education and subject being taught. This research presented a clear justification that the information found regarding SCL will lead to a practical application in the classroom and a critical examination, definition, and explanation of the most important factors relevant to this study.

This author found that there is extensive empirical evidence that supports a variety of instructional methods labeled as active student centered learning. This study also contains research of each learning/teaching method for evidence as to the value and effectiveness of each aspect that comprises student centered learning. It also cultivated effective ways to replace existing educational systems that do not optimize, and may actually diminish, student learning. (see handbook in appendix A).

The ideas and conclusions reached here are based solely on the conclusions arrived at by these researchers. I simply used their conclusions, perspective, experience, and knowledge in an attempt to present the results to teachers and instructors that is easy to understand and use in the classroom. It is hoped that instructors at all levels of education and experience will review and apply these ideas to improve student performance.

He used the knowledge and research of these very talented authors to analyze, synthesize, and draw conclusions based on reasoning and critical thinking to determine what would be most important and beneficial to what he was trying to accomplish.

In conclusion, the purpose or objective of this project is to provide the reader with an in-depth knowledge and understanding of the research regarding student-centered learning/teaching. The objective is to take these complex educational processes and simplify them as a means of assisting educators in teaching procedures that improve student performance in the classroom.

Introduction

This book began with an investigation to verify the research on each of the topics stated in order to establish a better understanding of the factors that drive these teaching methods, theories of learning as well as the effectiveness of each teaching method. This research found that there is beginning to be a tremendous support for the core elements of student-centered types of learning which is beginning to be universally accepted by many educators as an excellent and progressive approach to teaching/learning.

This book concentrates on student-centered learning (SCL), which encompasses active learning (AL), cooperative learning (COL), collaborative learning, (COLL) and occasionally constructivism learning (CONS) teaching methodologies.

Also included is a brief review of the theories of learning that provides insights into current research regarding the process of learning (how students learn) and a review of traditional/teacher-centered learning/teaching theories. This book is divided into six major sections. The first section is a brief review of several basic psychological and philosophical theories of learning. The second section is a summarized review of traditional/teacher-centered learning.

The third section is divided into four segments in which each segment contains a simple definition and explanation of the most used student-centered teaching philosophies and methodologies proposed for use in the classroom. Each of these topics contains a condensed definition and explanation of the basic philosophical and psychological theories and principles that construct these teaching strategies.

The fourth section contains thorough research into student-centered learning. The fifth section has three interactive student-centered learning (ISCL) segments; the first is a review of the process, the second covers an instructional development process and the third segment provides educators with a curriculum for organizing a program for teaching an (ISCL) curriculum. Appendix A contains a handbook that provides the teacher with knowledge/ information on how to develop an (ISCL) curriculum for teaching students effectively in almost all subjects at the secondary and college level.

Chapter One

The Learning Process

EDUCATIONAL LEARNING THEORIES

The main part of this chapter is divided into two sections. The first section provides a brief review and explanation of various theories of learning. Meanwhile, the second section is a summary of what these learning processes entail as they relate to education.

The relationship between learning theories and the educational process is complicated by many factors. It seems obvious that instructional practice would be based on the latest and best theories of learning. However, research indicates that educational practice is more likely to be based on past philosophical beliefs than on empirical evidence of the latest scientific studies that will provide for more efficient student learning.

Learning theories are conceptual frameworks that describe how information is absorbed, processed, and retained during the learning procedure. Emotional, cognitive, and prior experiences, in addition to environmental influences, appear to affect how understanding and knowledge are acquired or changed.

This book began as a study of various teaching methodologies, which, like learning theories, are numerous and frustrating when one is attempting to decide which theory (or theories) best fits with the teaching methods being used. This entry focuses on numerous conceptions and definitions of learning that have evolved over years of study and analysis. Although there are advantages and disadvantages of these theoretical perspectives, each theory will not be reviewed in great depth in this book, due to its limitation.

The main objective of this endeavor is to give educators a brief, simple appraisal of the main learning theories (which are extensive). A variety of learning theories will be presented. However, these theories, as the reader will discover, have some similar aspects but vary for a number of reasons. Teachers and students of educational psychology, curriculum development, and instructional methodology will find the information included beneficial.

A major purpose of the project is to assist educators in their study and understanding of the various learning theories, how they influence learning and how they can be applied to the major teaching methodologies. A teacher's perspective of learning should consist of curriculum content, academic achievement, readiness to learn, and the ability to transfer what is being learned to new or future situations.

This often includes social behavior and interactions and the knowledge that students can learn through conscious and deliberate effort. However, what teachers teach and students learn, understand, retain, and transfer to knowledge are skills that are often contrary to what should be taking place.

Because student learning is the very core of the educational process, educators must understand that effective learning is one of the most important endeavors in which students will engage. As the author began his research for information regarding learning theories, he discovered that there are a tremendous number of ideas/theories regarding the process of learning. The more he researched, the more he began to realize that the methods of teaching that correspond with various learning theories have been proposed only in the last half century or so.

Although several theories have dominated the educational process in the past, consideration must now be given to the new and advanced theories that are being recommended. Continued research and knowledge has moved forward with new scientific understandings of how students learn, retain information, and increase their knowledge.

To better understand the learning process, it became necessary to find a concrete definition of learning. Learning theories are conceptual frameworks that describe how information is absorbed, processed, and retained during learning. The following are several definitions that research has proposed: 1) the act or experiences acquired by the learner, 2) knowledge obtained by instruction and study, and 3) the modification of behavior by instruction and conditioning. Learning consists of a body of principles advocated by psychologists and educators to explain how students acquire skills, knowledge, and the thinking process to improve and accelerate their learning.

Many theories attempt to explain how students learn; however, even experts in the learning process and educators are not in complete agreement as to which is best. In the past, most research explained learning as a combination of two basic aspects: behaviorism and the cognitive theories of learning.

Since learning is based on the student's acquisition of new knowledge, it depends on memory and the ability to retain and recall information. Simply put, learning can be defined as a change in behaviors as a result of a student's experiences. Based on this explanation, instruction must include a student's previous experiences when promoting learning. Therefore, instructors and teachers must understand that a student's background will greatly influence the way he or she learns and that learning must be an active process, have a purpose, be many sided, and be based on prior experiences.

Although numerous learning theories have been proposed, there appears to be no complete agreement, in literature, by educators and scientists as to which theories are most comprehensive. However, new research has brought forth many new ideas of learning, some which will be explained briefly within this book. Nonetheless, over the years, psychological research has provided education with many contrasting theories and ideas of how learning takes place. First, let's review a short criticism of learning theories.

Critics of many learning theories state that there is no need for learning theories in that the attempt to understand the process of learning is based on the development of theories that create learning problems and inhibit personal freedom. Conversely, most learning theorists counteract critics by stating that learning theories create a means of critical thinking, problems solving, and decision making that arises in a transformation process and depends on a student's previous knowledge, assumptions, experiences, and the environments in which learning takes place.

Conceptions of Learning

According to recent research, learning theories are conceptual structures that convey how information is absorbed, processed, and retained during learning. Cognitive, emotional, and environmental factors and previous experiences are important in influencing students in the understanding of how learning is acquired, or changed, and allow new skills and knowledge to be achieved, while maintaining previously learned skills.

Understanding any theory calls for a clear idea of what the theory is trying to authenticate. When a specific statement is used, people usually presume everyone has a common understanding of what that declaration entails. Regrettably, this has not always been the case when educators are trying to understand the abundant theories of learning and their implications for education. It is beneficial to realize that the term "learning" may have a different meaning to other people and that it is used somewhat differently in dissimilar situations.

Even though most definitions of learning involve changes in a student's knowledge, behavior, ability in skill performance, or participation in an activity with other students, there is a considerable variation among educational learning theories about the description of this transformation.

It is difficult to comprehend the similarities and differences among the abundance of theories presented in the literature in that the various theories are relevant to different types of learning and are not necessarily incompatible with one another. Therefore, radically different theories are applicable to classroom learning even if they deal with different aspects of learning. Many researchers have grouped learning into the following four broad concepts that may contain more than one learning theory:

- behaviorism: observable human behavior;
- cognitive: authentically a mental/neurological process;
- humanistic: emotions and how they affect and play a role in learning;
- social: greater learning takes place in groups and other relationships.

The concept of behaviorism focuses on two classifications: information processing and social interaction. Social interaction gained prominence in the 1980s and puts forth that the learning and changes that occur in behaviors are a result of interaction between the student and the environment and other people. Students perceive each learning situation from unique and different points of view. Each individual student's prior experiences are different and place readiness to learn, and understand situations, in a different light.

There are two key assumptions that underlie the cognitive approach: first, that the memory system is an active organized processor of information, and second, that prior knowledge plays an important role in learning.

Cognitive theories consider how human memory works to promote learning and the need to understand the importance of perception and short- and long-term memory in the learning process. Research today considers that cognitive load and information processing play a role in influencing instructional design. The result is that cognitive theory is used to explain the importance of social role acquisition, intelligence and memory, and their effects on learning. Information theorists indicate that the brain's internal structures select and process incoming information to be stored in memory.

This information is available for retrieval in order to reproduce the behavior that receives and processes feedback. Information processing involves many cognitive procedures that include organization of data and planning and monitoring performance, in addition to encoding and chunking information. The result produces both internal and external responses (Baddeley1996).

Information processing, as a way of learning, is due to the acquisition of new information and the ability to use this data repeatedly through memory and recall. Simply put, learning takes place as students absorb, retain, and recall information for future use. Therefore, the student's information processing approach to learning indicates that learning occurs when students encounter new information and connect it to existing knowledge and prior experiences, which results in new knowledge.

This procedure requires that, after encoding, new information must be translated from perceptual experiences into representations in the mind where information can be put to use or stored in memory for future recall. However, numerous studies indicate that repeating information constantly is not an efficient way to learn. Research by Monisha Pasupathi (2002) suggests that continually reviewing notes is not an efficient learning process.

Learning studies have found that reading and thinking about how material can be connected to other items we already know and that using prior knowledge is a better means of learning. In addition, the more a learning method approximates the way information is going to be used and recalled, the more learning will be effective. Furthermore, continuous recall and retrieval of what students need to know strengthens what is remembered over time. The information process of constantly retrieving data from memory goes by the "use it or lose it rule."

Principles of Learning

Several principles of learning have been identified by educational psychologists that usually seem to relate to how students learn. The following factors provide brief insights into these principles:

- **Readiness:** Individuals learn when they want to learn. It is the teachers' responsibility to get students ready to learn.
- **Exercise**: Issues repeated continually are often those that are best learned.
- **Effect**: Issues are strengthened when events are pleasant and satisfying and weakened when unpleasant. So, make learning fun.
- **Primacy**: Events that are learned first become most impressive and retained but are difficult to change if they are wrong.
- **Regency**: The most recent events are the easiest to remember.
- **Perception**: The base of all learning is directed to the brain by one or more of the following five types of senses: visual, auditory, kinetic, smell, or taste.

Learning occurs fastest if more than one sense is used. Perceptual efficiency in learning is best achieved by reducing the task to be performed to its simplest and most productive form. Because information receiving involves differentiating, identifying, and recognizing from a variety of informational cues, learning must proceed from the most basic to the most difficult. More specifically, reception of a small number of stimuli creates the best learning conditions for acquisition or learning by simplifying the environment.

Learning is increased and more efficient if concise phrases or key words are used to explain the information to be learned. Reducing complex ideas to their simplest form prevents mental overload during learning, which leads to improved learning, enhanced retention, and the ability to recall information.

Theories of Forgetting

An important factor in learning is how the instructor controls the important problem of forgetting. Therefore, it should be mentioned that consideration must be given as to why students fail to remember information they have learned in the classroom. The following are the two main theories that account for forgetting:

- **Disuse**: This theory indicates that a student will forget information that is not used regularly. However, the information is still in the mind, but the difficulty in recalling or retrieving this data is what causes the problem of remembering.
- **Interference**: Experience/knowledge is forgotten by the student because new experience/knowledge tends to overshadow them. This interference distracts the remembrances of similar material and material not well learned.

To resolve the problem of forgetting, students must first learn the information or skill so completely that recall becomes easy or habitual; second, the student must recognize the types of situations where it is appropriate to use and involve the process of learning transfer. And last, the student needs to be reminded that in forgetting information, it is not really gone, but is still available for recall. Teaching what is to be learned thoroughly and with meaning, approval, association, the right attitude, using all the senses, and meaningful repetition will support remembering and impede forgetting.

LEARNING THEORIES

Conditioning

Behaviorism is a learning perspective that focuses on changing students' individual behavior, that is, what they say or do. Educational psychologist John Watson (1878–1959) proposed two major theories that include *behaviorism* (learning that creates changes) in overt behavior and *constructivism* (learning that changes students' thinking). The psychological effects of constructivism are a result of "thinking" as an individual experience and "social," when it changes thinking as a result of the action of others.

Behaviorism, as a learning experience, is the acquisition of new behaviors through conditioning. Classical conditioning is a process where behavior becomes a reflex response to a stimulus in the environment. Behaviorism articulates learning as a change in behavior, which is a characteristic of conditioning and based on a system of rewards and targets. There are two ways people learn by conditioning. *Classical* conditioning is where behavior becomes a reflex response to a stimulus and *operant* conditioning is where behavior is reinforcement by a reward or punishment.

Educational methodologies that are based on this approach to learning consist of applied behavior analysis, curriculum-based measurements, and direct instruction. The major components of behaviorism in learning consist of new associations that are made possible through prior experiences, and these new learning behaviors result in a change in learning. However, Watson (1924) believes that good thoughts, intentions, or other subjective experiences are unscientific and insists that psychology must focus on behaviors that are measurable.

Constructivism

The research of Jean Paiget and Jerome Bruner suggested the emphasis of constructivism is the result of the importance of what is accomplished by building new ideas and concepts, based on one's current knowledge and past experiences. Constructionists indicate that students do not learn deeply by listening to a teacher or reading a textbook. According to constructivists, educators must design an effective teaching environment built on what students already know. Thus, they believe that teachers need a thorough understanding of what students know and develop a curriculum based on this knowledge. However, a problem arises in that what students know varies among students.

Cognitive Theories

Gestalt psychologists provide demonstrations and describe principles to explain the way people organize their impressions into perceptions. Gestalt psychologists censure behaviorists for being too dependent on overt behavior to explain learning. They propose looking at the patterns that occur rather than at isolated events. Gestalt views of learning have been incorporated into what has become labeled as *cognitive theories*.

Two key assumptions underlie this cognitive approach: first, that the memory system is an active organized processor of information and second, that prior knowledge plays an important role in learning. Cognitive theories look beyond behavior to consider how human memory works to promote learning; and an understanding of short-term memory and long-term memory is important to educators who are influenced by cognitive theory.

They view learning as an internal mental process (including insight, information processing, memory, and perception) where the educator must focus on building intelligence and cognitive development. After memory theories like the Atkinson-Shiffrin's Memory Model and Baddeley's working Memory Model, became established as a theoretical framework in cognitive psychology, new cognitive frameworks of learning began to emerge during the 1970s, 1980s, and 1990s.

Today, researchers concentrate on topics such as cognitive load and information processing as theories of learning that play a role in influencing instructional design, while cognitive theory is used to explain topics such as social role acquisition, intelligence, and memory as related to age.

Educators who are supportive of a cognitive theory of learning believe that the definition of learning, as a change in behavior, is too narrow and prefer to study the learner and base learning on the apparent complexities of human memory, rather than his or her environment. Cognitive research indicates that the two key assumptions that underlie the cognitive approach are 1) the memory system plays an active role as an organized processor of information, and 2) that prior knowledge plays an important role in learning. A simple explanation of memory is that it accepts and inputs data and stimuli to be processed from an external source, which are then placed in storage so that they can be recalled at a later date.

Cognitive theories look beyond behavior to consider how human memory works in promoting learning and are based on an understanding that short-term memory and long-term memory are important to educators who are influenced by cognitive theory. These scientists view learning as an internal mental process (including insight, information processing, memory, and perception) where the educator focuses on building intelligence and cognitive development. In this learning situation the individual learner is more important than the environment.

EVOLVING THEORIES OF LEARNING

Modern theories of learning are based on the psychological studies that began with Herman Ebbinghaus's study of memory (1850–1909), Edward Thorndike's (1874–1949) dissertation on problem solving, and Pavlov's (1849–1936) classic conditioning theories that focus on explaining human behavior as based on behavior theories. Their work is based on stimulus/response as an explanation of learning. These behavioral theorists focus on environmental factors, including feedback, reinforcement, and practice, to indicate that learning occurs externally.

However, educators tend to overlook these and other learning theories and base their conclusion on philosophical understanding rather than empirical evidence as a theoretical understanding of learning. The following learning theories are gradually being accepted and will become important in the future. In the 1990s, dubbed the "Decade of the Brain," huge advances were achieved in neuroscience and in how the brain interacts with human behavior to produce learning. In addition to having a huge influence on future learning, these evolving studies greatly added to education's understanding of how humans learn.

Educational Neuroscience

These research studies seek to link an understanding of how the brain processes information with classroom instruction and experiences. The objective of neuroscience is to analyze the biological changes that take place in the brain when information is processed. This is achieved as science looks at which environmental, emotional, and social situations are best suited for information to be retained and stored in the brain via the linking of neurons, rather than allowing the dendrites to absorb information before it is lost.

The integration into, and application to, education of what science knows about the brain was advanced in 2000 when the American Federation of Teachers concluded: "It is vital that we identify what science puts forth about how students learn, in order to improve the educational curriculum." Although the field of neuroscience is young, it is believed that with new technologies and ways of observing, learning will provide the standards that students need to improve their learning, will be further refined, and based on actual scientific evidence.

American universities such as Harvard, Johns Hopkins, the University of Southern California, and other academic institutions, in the first decade of the twenty-first century, began offering majors and degrees dedicated to educational neuroscience or neuro-education. These studies search for links to understand how the brain processes classroom instruction and experiences. Neuro-education seeks to analyze the biological changes that occur in the brain as recent information is dealt with. This procedure looks at which environmental, emotional, and social situations are best for retaining and storing new information in the brain, so that the information is not lost.

The 1990s were designated "the Decade of the Brain," as progress took place in neuroscience at an exceptionally rapid pace. The three dominant methods for measuring brain activities are: event-related potential, functional magnetic resonance imaging and MEG (brain mapping).

What is exciting about this advanced field in education is that modern brain imaging techniques now make it possible, in some sense, to watch the brain as it learns.

Although the field of neuroscience is young, it is assumed that with innovative technologies and ways of observing learning, the model of what students need and how students learn best will be further refined, with actual scientific evidence. As an example, students who may have learning disabilities will be taught with strategies that are more informed.

In brain-based theories of learning, there are differences of opinion in psychological theories that indicate the learning process is not yet completely understood. Neuroscience shows that the brain can be modeled, not as a central processor where "intelligence" lies, but in having perhaps seventy functional areas, allowing mental activity to take place as several areas work together. What appears as different types of intelligence results from different combinations of well-developed functional areas. Learning is a process by which neurons are joined by developing the synapses between them. Knowledge is arranged hierarchically, with additional knowledge being linked to existing neural networks.

Transformative Learning Theory

This theory seeks to explain how humans revise and reinterpret meaning. Transformative learning is the cognitive process that affects change in a frame of reference as it defines our view of the world. Emotions often become involved, in that adults have a tendency to reject any ideas that do not correspond to their particular values, associations, or concepts.

Our frame of reference is composed of two dimensions: habits of mind and points of view. Habits of mind, such as ethnocentrism, are harder to change than points of view. Habits of mind influence our point of view and the resulting thoughts or feelings associated with them, but points of view may change over time as a result of influences such as reflection, appropriation, and feedback.

Transformative learning takes place by discussing with others the reasons presented in support of competing interpretations, by critically examining evidence, arguments, and alternative points of view. When circumstances permit, transformative learners move toward a frame of reference that is more inclusive, discriminating, self-reflective, or integrative of experiences.

Multiple Intelligences

Psychologist Howard Gardner's research (1999) suggests that there are in existence multiple intelligences and that several dissimilar kinds of intelligence exist in people. There has been a continuous process of professional development in the study of the development of human intelligence. Gardner's Multiple Intelligences Theory suggests that there are at least seven ways that people have for perceiving and understanding the world. Gardner labels each of these characteristics as distinct "intelligences," in other words, a set of skills allowing individuals to find and resolve genuine problems that learners encounter in the environment.

Gardner further defines intelligence as a group of abilities that are somewhat independent from other human capacities, in that intelligence has a core set of information-processing operations based on the distinct stages of development that students pass through in the learning process. This process takes place probably because it has plausible roots in evolutionary history. These seven theories are not included here due to book limitations but can be found on the Internet under *Gardner's theories of learning*.

Multimedia Learning

The use of visual and auditory teaching materials may include video, computer, and other information technology. Multimedia learning theory focuses on the principles that determine the effective use of multimedia in learning, with emphasis on using both the visual and auditory channels for information processing.

The auditory learning channel deals with information that is heard, and the visual channel processes information that is seen. The auditory channel holds more information than the visual channels. However, if both the auditory and visual channels are presented with information, more knowledge is retained. Conversely, if too much formation is delivered and inadequately processed, it will not be established in long-term memory. Multimedia learning seeks to give instructors the ability to stimulate both the auditory and visual channels of the learner, resulting in a sound learning progression.

Learning Styles

This theory proposes that if the student and educators know a learner's style of learning, it will lead to faster and more satisfactory improvement in learning. The learning style theory indicates that individuals learn in different ways and that knowledge of a learner's preferred learning style will lead to faster and more satisfactory improvement. Additional data about learning styles and a learning style survey can be found in appendix D.

FACTORS THAT AFFECT LEARNING

Studies in learning have developed several factors that affect a student's ability to learn. They are:

- **Motivation**: has been determined to be the predominant force that manages students' progress and ability to learn. Therefore, negative feedback must be abolished in order to reinforce the positive desire for personal gain.
- **Self-Concept**: a potent determinant in student learning that inspires confidence and safety.
- **Time and Opportunity:** the awareness that the availability of time affords students with the perception that they have the capability and opportunity to complete assignments.

- **Perception**: involves the acceptance of stimuli from the five senses and affects how a student reacts and provides meaning to awareness.
- **Basic Need**: the process that maintains and enhances the organized self to help the student to preserve and maintain who they are.
- **Goals and Values**: the philosophical aspects that students must embrace: it is essential for instructors to know that this knowledge will assist in determining how students interpret their educational experiences and instruction.
- **The Element of Threat:** Fear is a main factor in a student's learning in that it can negatively affect how a student becomes aware of an object or condition that occurs.
- **Insight:** The instructor's foremost responsibility is the student's response to new experiences.

THE ART OF TEACHING AND LEARNING

Although the role of the teacher as a facilitator (someone who make learning, or an activity, easier to accomplish) is covered in each chapter of the book as it relates to that aspect of student learning, Patrick Allitt (2010) has developed some important methods a teachers can use as a means of improving student learning, especially at the college level.

He believes that teachers must be hired based on their ability, educational training, and understanding of how students learn best. Good teaching is improved when teachers are self-critical of their own teaching and are willing to except new theories and teaching methods regarding how students learn.

As facilitators of learning, teachers must provide students with the tools for self-learning, establish positive impression about the learning process, and develop relationships with the class as well as individual students. The relationship and interaction between student and teacher should be practical, intellectual, and gratifying.

Remember, positive first impressions about the teacher, the process of learning, and the content being studied are a very important issue, and they can be enhanced by the teacher's displaying interest in the class and subject matter being taught. The facilitator can develop student interest in learning by instituting the following practices:

- Learn each student's name.
- Plan the class introduction.
- Display your expertise in the subject matter being taught by discussing the content to be presented.
- Indicate that class and student success is import to you.
- Emphasize what you expect of the class.

- Add humor to the class whenever possible.
- Discuss the assignments and type of work required to succeed.
- Create an environment that increases student curiosity and interest and engages students.
- Outline and explain the rules the students must follow to succeed.
- Insist that students come to their class and their groups on time and be well prepared.

Patrick Allitt, a professor at Emory University and a contributor to Great Courses with his introduction to student learning concluded that teachers and students need to cultivate good learning experiences in remembering (learning) the most important issues. In the long term students must learn to self-teach in order to push themselves into the learning zone that points students in the right direction. Self-learning is an important aspect of student learning due to the constant and rapid changes taking place in life and new ways of learning that require problem solving and the development of critical thinking ability.

Students must learn not to depend on the teacher to supply all their learning needs. This includes not only learning from the teacher but also learning from their peers. Professor Allitt concluded that students learn best when they are active and in small groups that use their experiences and that are managed to improve the learning process and increase knowledge. Because learning is hard work, teachers must give students the tools for learning that include the ability to read and understand what they have read. Studies in neurosciences are constantly changing ideas about the learning process and what educators can expect from students.

Parents are first in the learning chain with teachers following and finally the student who must take responsibility for their learning experiences. Self-learning becomes an important aspect of student learning in that events in life are rapidly changing and new ways of learning are constantly evolving. Therefore, by developing critical thinking ability students learn to not depend on their teacher or parent to provide all their learning needs. Generally, there is no limit to what students can learn. What must happen is to create students who enjoy the learning process.

In addition, the more students learn, the more they want to learn what they don't know, which increases their desire to learn. Students must discover that learning is a lifelong, active process that is practical and intellectual and that, at the same time, takes place in an environment that is influenced by such factors as:

- a student's daily experiences;
- intellectual ability;
- health issues that can affect the learning process;

- personality;
- complexity and the constant change in social interactions;
- different learning abilities, styles, and thoughts among students;
- the number of words heard per day (the greater the number, the more improvement in learning);
- will power/self control; and
- different methods of learning/teaching.

The following learning tricks (brain exercises) that will advance the learning process can be used:

- hands-on learning that requires project management and team work;
- increased education;
- curiosity and the ability to challenge students;
- hobbies/travel;
- learning a new language;
- patterned puzzles;
- aerobic exercise, which protects the brain; and
- multitasking.

KEY IDEAS TO REMEMBER

As theories of learning have evolved over the past half century, definitions of learning have shifted from changes that occur in the mind or behavior of an individual to changes that occur while participating in ongoing activities with other individuals. This process could change a person's identity within a group (e.g., a change from being a follower, to being a leader). Although most definitions of learning involve a change in an individual's knowledge or ability to perform a skill or participate in an activity with other individuals, there is considerable variation among the theories about the nature of this change.

Further difficulty in understanding similarities and differences among various concepts results from the recurring overlooked fact that there are different types of learning. In any case, the various theories are relevant to different types of learning and are not necessarily incompatible with one another. Preferably, they provide diverse perspectives on the complex phenomena of learning and complement one another in their ability to explain different types of learning circumstances. Thus, radically different theories can be made relevant to the classroom by addressing different aspects of classroom learning.

Therefore, it is wise to avoid comparing apples with oranges. It's no secret that students learn best when they self-regulate and set their own academics. Self-regulation strategies will assist students in goal achievement and reflect on academic performance. Educators should know that students learn through communication, discussion, and argumentation. Therefore, educational methods must make use of these factors that develop cognitive restructuring and of informed curriculum development. This strategy promotes the use of prior knowledge to help students gain a broad understanding and development of new learning concepts.

The reality of it all is that the relationship between theory and practice is a two-way street, due to the belief that knowledge arises from sound scientific theories of learning that determine effective educational practices. However, science does function in a linear fashion in that learning often comes from observing and questioning things as they occur in the real world. This premise further aligns with the idea that teaching concepts and the language of a subject should be divided into multiple steps. Other informed learning theories look at the sources of motivation for learning that include intrinsic motivation that may create more self-regulated learners. Yet, schools tend to undermine intrinsic motivation.

Critics argue that the average student, who learns in isolation, performs at a significantly lower level than those learning through collaboration and mediation. Some educators believe they can help students develop learning strategies through their teaching. Others, however, don't think it's their place to do so and point to the load of content they must already teach during the semester. Learning theories have often been used to provide a guide for education and educators.

Earlier applications were concerned with the use of appropriate rewards and punishment that mirror the major principles of behaviorist theories. More recently, cognitive perspectives have shaped the field of education in that there is more concern with learning methods that enhance long-term retention, transfer of information, and skill development. For example, using variability in encoding and learning material in different ways (e.g. video and text) will produce more durable long-term retention,

In addition, students can become better thinkers when they receive specific instruction in thinking skills and when the instruction is designed to enhance transfer. Teaching strategies that enhance transfer include spaced practice (viewing material over time versus cramming), using a variety of examples so learners can recognize where a concept is appropriate, and practice at retrieval (recovery of learning over time) with informative feedback.

Learning theories are facing innovative challenges as people grapple with increases in the large amount of available information that needs to be learned, rapidly changing technologies that require new types of responses to different problems, and the need to continue learning throughout one's life. Contemporary learning theories supported by empirical research offer the promise of enhanced learning and improved thinking—both which are critical in a rapidly changing and complex world.

Finally, perceptual efficiency in learning is best achieved by reducing the tasks to be performed to their simplest and most productive form. Because information receiving involves differentiating, identifying, and recognizing a variety of informational cues, learning must proceed from the most basic to the most difficult (keep it simple, Stupid). More specifically, reception of small numbers of stimuli creates the best conditions for learning acquisition by simplifying the environment. Learning is further increased and more efficient if concise phrases or key words are used to explain the information to be learned.

For example, when designing learning procedures, large amounts of information must be dealt with gradually from the simple to the complex. Brevity is best, in that the reduction of complex ideas to their simplest form prevents mental overloading during learning, thereby improving the form of what is to be learned while enhancing retention and recall ability.

"Mental exhaustion" caused by extremely long periods of study that produce fatigue should be limited so that learning is not restricted. Several short periods of study are generally better than one long period, while studying that ends on a positive note during a peak learning period produces the best results. The following chapters of this book begin with a description of a traditional approach to learning followed by five student-centered learning methodologies, which consists of active, cooperative, collaborative, constructionist, and student-centered approaches. The book's major purpose ends with a review of interactive student-centered cooperative, collaborative, and constructivist approaches to learning.

Chapter Two

Traditional Learning/Teaching

The objective of this chapter is to review the positive and negative aspects of traditional learning, in order to enable teachers and administrators to make sound and educated decisions as to the effectiveness of traditional teaching methodologies in the modern educational system.

Traditional education, often referred to as *conventional education* or *back-to-the-basics education*, is a teaching/learning process that has been deemed by society as an appropriate learning process. The major objective of this book is not to ridicule traditional education or the lecturing process. The purpose is to use it as a means of distributing information covering an outdated approach to education and the learning process. There is an old but timely Chinese proverb that goes like this: "Tell me and I'll forget; show me and I may remember; involve me and I'll understand."

For many students learning requires more than listening to a lecture or seeing a presentation in order to process and remember information. Utilizing interactive procedures and student-centered learning techniques may be, for many students, the difference between learning and failure in education.

The traditional classroom begins with a learning process that emphasizes basic skills and a strict adherence to a fixed curriculum that includes textbooks and lectures. In traditional learning, the instructor presents knowledge while students receive it as the instructor assumes a directive and authoritative role. Assessment occurs via testing student work individually, based on correct answers on tests that evaluate knowledge achievement.

The following criticism by progressive educators regarding traditional learning, or teacher-centered learning (TCL), states that it is comprised of a teacher/instructor-centered methodology, style or theory of learning, in which the teacher delivers knowledge in the form of information. Thus, traditional learning contains passive learning by the students from lectures or an occasional discussion dominated by the instructor. In the process of TCL the teacher distributes information to students who are now responsible for comprehending and managing what is being presented. Students do not work cooperatively but in competition with one another.

Many educational institutions use a defined curriculum, in an instructor-centered environment, which allows the instructor to control the learning material, the learning process, and the pace of learning where students achieve and memorize knowledge. On occasion students in TCL are involved in individual discussion that takes place between students and instructor. If the teacher/instructor is lecturing and he or she is a good lecturer and communicator of information, students may leave class believing that they know and understand information and may even retain information presented during the lecture: research shows that only 5 percent of lecture information is retained.

However, on occasion the instructor or students asks questions that are almost always answered or engaged in by only a few of the same students who asked the questions. In addition, class assignments such as projects and worksheets are most often researched and done individually.

Research indicates that hands-on activities, such as group discussion, questioning; projects and other learning techniques create higher levels of student learning and data retention.

Wikipedia.com states that the teacher-centered (traditional) learning methods that focus on rote learning and memorization must take a more holistic approach to learning and focus more on student-centered learning. Studies by Udovic, Morris, Dickman, Postlewait, and Weherwax (2002) indicate that the TCL approach may not provide students with significant learning skills or a body of knowledge that will last beyond the end of the semester.

They concluded that in order to enhance the quality of teaching and learning nontraditional methodologies such as active, collaborative, cooperative, and problem-based learning must be employed. However, according to Herreid (1998) and the experiences of Harris and Johnson, teachers who are not trained in establishing nontraditional goals and objectives have difficulty implementing student learning methodologies and assessment techniques and are likely to be ineffective when utilizing these strategies in the classroom.

Therefore, traditional faculty members have been driven to continue teaching with TCL-based lecture methods, making it difficult for progressive teaching methods to be successfully instilled. In order for supporters of non-teacher-centered learning to install a progressive form of teaching, the instructors must reflect on their personal goals, student goals, student needs, and the level and purpose of what is to be taught. In addition, according to Tanenbaum, Cross, Tilsons, and Rogers (1998) instructors must consider the specific knowledge, skills and attitudes of each student if progressive education is to be successful.

Furthermore, they concluded that the student-centered learning (SCL) process is difficult in a classroom with an extremely large number of students. In conclusion, Wikipedia.com states that traditional education focuses on teaching, not learning and that this learning process erroneously presumes every minute spent in teaching is a minute of student learning. Critics also argue that the learning taking place in TCL is soon forgotten, while what is remembered is often irrelevant.

THE OBJECTIVES OF TCL

An instructor in a teacher-directed class must express his or her approach to learning that recognizes what students should be required to institute in order to achieve their goals and set realistic expectations. The primary concern of TCL is to convey to the next generation those skills, facts, knowledge, and standards of moral and social conduct that have been found to be necessary to improve society. Therefore, teachers are appointed to communicate knowledge and enforce the desired and required standards of behavior. This approach, which was imported from Europe, dominated the American education scene well into the nineteenth century, until various forms of progressive education were introduced into education—again from Europe.

The reason chalk-and-talk learning remains in use is that it is seen to be a relatively efficient, and less expensive, method of imparting information quickly and to a large body of students. In order to attain a solid TCL learning foundation, the following factors are used to justify TCL.

- Students work individually to achieve curricular objectives in order to become critical thinkers.
- Students complete activities designed by the teacher to achieve academic success.
- Students respond to positive expectations set by the teacher as they progress through activities.
- Students are given extrinsic motivators like grades and rewards that are supposed to motivate students and internalize information.
- Students must develop the ability to objectively demonstrate their understanding of concepts presented. Student work is evaluated by the teacher and focuses on independent learning where socializing is generally discouraged.

Benefits

Research indicates that the benefits of teacher-centered or traditional learning are extremely limited when related to more advanced learning methodologies. However, teachers and some research support traditional learning because of the benefits listed below:

- Teachers are considered experts who provide a knowledge base that can be imparted to students.
- Teachers assume full responsibility for course planning, execution, and achievement.
- Teachers are better able to discipline student behavior.
- Teachers control evaluations and student assessments.
- Teachers are better able to plan course procedures and the direction of learning.
- Students must be taught self-discipline at an early age.
- The pace of learning will be evident and testing can be instigated at the proper time.
- Traditional learners are more at ease in this type of learning environment.

Disadvantages

A major principle of good learning is that learning is not a spectator sport, in that students do not learn much just sitting in a class room listening to the teacher while memorizing prepackaged assignments and trying to spit out the answer. Critics, such as H. Greenberg, (1987), state that what is taught in the traditional classroom situation is soon forgotten, and most of what students remember is irrelevant. President Woodrow Wilson, who became a university professor, once stated upon leaving a history class after a test, "I am glad that is over and I won't have to remember that information anymore."

The teaching methods used in traditional education are generally composed of lectures where students learn by direct instruction (listening to lectures), by observation, reading textbooks, and individually written assignments, provide the focal point that determines a learners success. Therefore, the level of achievement is determined according to objective individual performance in which a passing grade often may not significantly lead to increased knowledge. Students of TCL often do well on tests and written assignments but fail to understand or retain information.

Armstrong (2002) stated that traditional education disregards and restrains learner responsibility that is found in student-centered learning. The following is a list of traditional learning factors that Armstrong indicated may hinder the learning process.

- Traditional education focuses on teaching and not learning

- Teaching fails to focus on exploration and experimentation and reinforce lifelong learning skills.
- It places emphasis on standards, curriculum and passing tests instead of student-focused learning. Motivation for learning must be based on intrinsic rewards.
- Learning is based on repetition and memorization of facts which reduce retention rates and lower test scores
- It lacks emphasis on the critical thinking skills gained through experience, reasoning, and the ability to apply complicated concepts to lifelong learning.
- Too much emphasis is placed on passing tests, regardless of fact that students may not understand testing material.
- Students do not develop a deep level of knowledge that is required for understanding complex concepts.
- It fails to improve oral, written, and listening communication skills.
- It proposes a single, unified curriculum for all students regardless of their ability or interest.
- Little or no attention is spent on social development.

Teachers' Role

In the traditional classroom, students are generally placed in a class based on their age, sometimes by ability, and are all taught the same material. The teaching methods used in traditional-teacher learning consist of direct instruction, lectures, and desk work and through listening and observation. Instruction is generally based on textbooks, lectures, and individual written assignments. The primary role of the teacher is to assign and present information for students to study and memorize at school or in home assignments. This process creates an extremely inefficient use of student and teacher time. The following is an outline of factors that pertain to the TCL teacher's role in educating students:

- Novak's (1998) studies indicate that in traditional teaching the teacher was the cause of all learning that occurs.
- Emphasis is placed on the teacher as a knowledge dispenser and the students as repositories of learning.
- The major objective is to make learning interesting and fun.
- It fits the difficulty of task being studied to the skills of the student.
- In traditional learning the teacher is held in high esteem and must be obeyed by all students.

Assessment

Assessment is the tool that tells how well students are achieving their learning outcomes. The first thing that should to be determined is what students need to know and be able to do as a result of what they have been taught. This begins by reviewing the goals and objectives that have been set by the instructor. In establishing assessment procedures, the instructor often fails to take into account the effects of previous knowledge and a student's learning style. Evaluation and assessment should be above reproach and an ongoing process in which evaluation is continuous throughout the entire learning procedure.

The process of achieving their goals, as well as the product of their learning environment should also be evaluated. The process of assessment in TCL include tests or oral examinations that are generally given at end of each unit being studied and that rely on reciting what the student has studied and memorized.

Grades or marks may be assigned according to objective individual performance, usually by the number of correct answers to a test or other measuring devices. However, passing may or may not signify expertise of the subject or skill being taught. Often students complete the assigned tasks but may not understand the material. Achievement must be based on performance that is compared to a reasonable standard.

The most important element of assessing performance is to engage and engross student in the challenge of learning. This requires the ability to learn by doing and communicating with others what they have learned. The following is a list of factors that will enable the instructor to verify if learning has taken place:

- Were students allowed equal opportunities to perform?
- Were the student required to use critical learning thinking and problem-solving skills?
- Was evaluation ongoing throughout the assignment?
- Were the students able to achieve the goals they established?
- The traditional approach requires that all students be taught the same materials at the same time

Students and teachers need to understand that assessment and evaluation is a process that evaluates student's performance generally at the end of the project and should consist of the three main learning components: content, the process, and the project. Students should understand that evaluation is a performance-based generative and ongoing process in which students will be given multiple opportunities to display what they have learned.

In the traditional learning process, the teacher/instructor is the primary source of knowledge, and the motivation for learning is to gain information that is presented by the teacher/instructor to the student. This process provides the rational for rote learning and memorization of notes and lectures presented by the teacher, which has become and educational norm. In today's educational methodologies, student-centered classrooms are preferred, and active learning is strongly encouraged.

As research shows, students excel kinesthetically by means that include experiencing the material they need to learn, by touching and feeling, and through cooperative learning that encourages interaction between the student, the instructor, and the information to be studied. Several studies indicate that students prefer a nontraditional approach to learning. Moreover, research of cooperative learning at the college level reported higher test scores in active and cooperative learning classes than in traditional learning process.

LEARNING VERSUS STUDENT-CENTERED LEARNING

Teaching has been defined as the ability to impart knowledge and develop competence by giving instructions, study, and experiences. However, imparting knowledge or skills does not ensure the acquisition of wisdom. For years teachers have taught with students being responsible for learning the material presented by the teacher.

It is arguable that much of today's education is based on outdated educational theories and philosophy that may no longer be effective. Discourse is constantly put forth that it is not enough to merely teach when the most important element is student education. It has become obvious that teaching and learning are not necessarily synonymous with one another. It is necessary to understand that just being an expert in a field of study and presenting a set of material in an organized manner does not necessarily mean that learning is taking place. Learning is a skill or ability that enables students to attain and retain knowledge.

According to some studies, problems occur in traditional teaching because student needs and readiness levels have changed considerably, and education is not always meeting these changing needs. For today's education to be successful, the needs of students must be met by changes in the teaching and learning process. Many psychologists indicate that a teacher-centered learning philosophy dictates that student learning is the primary goal of teaching, as opposed to learning and education being the main objective.

The following are several areas in which SCL (student-centered learning) differs from TCL. In SCL:

- Students are grouped by interest and ability.
- Project-based instruction is used (using any resource available).
- Significant attention is given to social development that includes, teamwork, interpersonal relationships, and self-awareness.
- Students can choose or be directed toward different kinds of classes according to perceived abilities.
- All students must achieve a basic level of education or spend extra time in school.

Conversely, a student-centered philosophy establishes that the teacher must assume the responsibility as facilitator of student learning. This process requires the teacher to be a motivating force in student learning, participation, thinking critically, problem solving, and performing successfully in evaluations and assessments. This procedure shifts the responsibility for learning to the student.

KEY IDEAS TO REMEMBER

Today's student needs and readiness level have changed considerably, challenging and creating obstacles that often hinder student academic success. These changing needs of students require the education system and teaching to effectively seek solutions that meet these essential needs. Likewise, research indicates that a transition must be made to student-centered learning as the main approach to educating students.

In this book, several learning theories, strategies, and methodologies of learning will be presented.

The book begins with a review of the learning process and traditional learning. In addition, an in-depth review of active learning, cooperative learning, collaborative learning, constructive learning, and student-centered learning is included. The book concludes with interactive student-centered learning (ISCL) that includes the process and instructional development of ISCL and presents most of the factors that establish an interactive student-centered teaching course of study

If learning is to be most effectively achieved, these traditional factors must be reviewed. The same is true for the educational activities that take place in the traditional classroom that revolve around, and are controlled by, the teacher, who dictates the type of learning activities that occur and who engage students in the learning process by presenting the material and knowledge to be learned.

Chapter Three

Active Learning

Neuroscience now supports active learning as the way people naturally learn. Active learning is a most effective method for creating knowledge through experimental learning. Active learning (AL) engages and expands student's educational experiences by providing for exploration, thinking, reflection, and interaction in a learning environment. This process allows real-life experiences to influence learning in a simple, effective, and easy educational approach that is based on a firm foundation in research and just plain common sense.

In equating active learning with traditional learning, Louis Deslaurieas (2011) concluded from his research that AL teaching is a process that uses a wide range of educational strategies that make it possible for students to actively take part in the learning process and allows students to use active techniques to react, respond, and select information for processing. Students also come to class better prepared and pay closer attention during class activities because they may be called upon to participate at any time. Furthermore, students are more personally engaged in listening, which leads to asking more questions, more discussions, and more thinking.

Deslaurieas also listed the following learning factors that do not usually occur during traditional learning:

- Students were twice as engaged and scored twice as high on evaluations.
- Student attendance increased.
- Interaction increased interest that improved the learning environment.
- The way students learned appeared to be more efficient.

In the field of education, AL is often perceived of as a radical change from traditional education. Regardless, forms of active learning have begun to attract progressive educators who are looking for complementary alternatives to traditional education. The content of this book is, first, to offer several definitions for AL and second, to review a variety factors that make up this form of education. However, the lecture method may be an effective method for transmitting information but is lacking if the instructor is trying to convey knowledge.

Dr. Louis Abrahamson (2003) indicates that most educators know there are tremendous numbers of methodologies and philosophies regarding education and how learning should be accomplished. All have been highly researched and written about and are good, effective approaches to student learning and education. However, almost all teachers do some form of the active learning. Probably, one of the most effective learning processes is a combination of lecture and AL teaching if the instructor's objective is to pass on factual information and create student involvement.

However, there are many different styles and methods of teaching AL that may not be suitable for all situations. Perhaps, the type of teaching strategies used in the classroom should accomplish content goals with active engagement by the student/s. This can be realized by focusing less on the instructor's presentation of information and more on student self-learning activities. Over the past twenty years, research in cognitive learning has produced a lot of data regarding how people learn. The central tenet of this research has been generally accepted, in that everything that students learn is constructed by themselves.

Thus, it was concluded that in order for the brain to accept information, it must look for connections and interpret and understand what is being offered: otherwise, no outside source will have any effect on learning. Therefore, the instructor must understand that the brain is a learning mechanism in which the process is only indirectly related to the teacher and teaching. Abrahamson indicates that the following are possible causes why students fail to learn:

- Student failed to understand the crucial concept put forth by the instructor, which caused the information presented not to be understood.
- The student missed previous information presentations or did not understand the information that was presented. Therefore, the conceptual structures for learning were nonexistent.
- The student lacked interest, motivation, or the desire to expend the mental effort in developing a point of view and knowledge.

The inability of the instructor to interact with students creates a deficiency in the instructor's ability to understand whether learning has taken place. Active learning is a two-way process in which the learner will interact with the instructor, peers, and with other resources. Therefore, research has concluded that it is not possible to teach effectively without interaction.

Abrahamson further indicated that there are three guidelines for good active teaching and learning: The first step is the "summative" factor that requires the instructor to determine what information exists in the brains of their students, The second step is a "formative" function in which the instructor directs the students' mental processing through the assigned tasks that enable students to mentally construct those properties the instructor is trying to teach, and the third factor is developing the "motivation" that allow students to react at the right moment.

The development of small groups who work together in solving problems not only improves motivation, in addition to increasing knowledge structures and the ability to stay on the right track. Learning is hard work and the introduction of motivation when needed will make a difference in achieving performance and learning. For example, a task or lesson that offers challenges that give students something to think about and immediate feedback from their peers as well as the facilitator will act as a strong motivator and help maintain attention to the activity taking place.

As previously mentioned, a fundamental opinion put forth by cognitive science is that everything that people learn they construct for themselves. Therefore, no external force can have a direct effect on what students learn. Furthermore, if the brain does not take in information, look for connections, interpret this information so that it makes sense, no outside influence will have any effect on learning. In conclusion, since the brain is doing the learning, teaching and the teachers have only an indirect effect on learning. The end result is that, for the teacher, without interacting with the students, he or she has no way of knowing if the students truly understand what is being presented.

This happens because students may not understand crucial concepts being presented, or may have missed prior information, due to lack of motivation, interest and/or the desire to learn. A positive learning culture that foster confidence and respect enables learners to give and accept constructive criticism while seeing errors as stepping-stones to success. Instruction that addresses a variety of learning styles creates high expectations and allows time for the learner to think will have a tremendous effect on learning

DEFINITIONS

Active learning is a method of instruction that launches students on the path to learning that compels them to do meaningful learning activities. In short, it compels students to take an active part in and think about what they are doing. Interactive learning is a process that allows students to experience learning situations firsthand while giving them reliable and trustworthy knowledge. This method of instruction enables students to acquire, act upon, and test new knowledge. However, students who often attempt to learn new information find it unclear and need further explanation. This is where the instructor becomes a facilitator of learning.

Active learning as defined in this book pertains to learning that is hands on with students interacting with other students, outside resources, technology, and the facilitator. This process enables students to achieve a higher level of learning and is more effective because of the varying ways in which information and knowledge are delivered and learned. The instructor communicates personally back and forth with students regarding problems with their assignments. This method consists of any process where instructors assign projects, questions, and problems to solve that the students must research inside and outside the classroom with other students and then to be reviewed in class.

Active learning is a learning process where student learning is improved by the utilization of the AL approach to learning. In the AL process, subject matter includes audio, visual, kinesthetic and hands on learning styles. Thus, subject matter is made interactive when lessons teach the material to be learned while creating students interest and curiosity. The key to social learning is for students to learn to think critically about what he or she is trying to learn (knowledge) as a means of improving how to organize this information for learning groups and future classroom experiences.

Active learning is a simple and easy way to use teaching methods that have a solid foundation in research and common sense. It is a straightforward and effective teaching approach to learning, in which students work in an interactive environment that is based on their imagination. Active methods of learning require an exchange of thoughts, ideas, information, and knowledge of the techniques involved in interactive participation by students.

Research

Research by Bonwell and Edison (1991) found that active learning was comparable to the lecture process for achieving content mastery but superior to the lecture method for developing thinking and writing skills. Armstrong's (1983–2012) studies indicate that students learned better when actively engaged in the learning process, which includes writing papers, problem solving, and experimenting. Instructors can help student prepare better for the outside world by the utilization of an interactive learning approach to achieving knowledge in which students are actively engaged and participate in self-education.

This process will enable students to remember lessons learned and develop the ability to transfer this newly acquired knowledge and information into different situations from what is already learned. It is not only the acquisition of knowledge that is important but the processes by which facts are learned that will carry over to other environments.

Louis Deslaurier's research at the University of British Columbia found that AL teaching methods significantly increased student attendance and doubled both engagement and learning in the classes studied as compared to traditional learning. He concluded that there is overwhelming evidence that teaching pedagogy based on cognitive psychology greatly improves student learning. Although the students had to work harder, they felt that they learned more and were more vested in their own learning

A research study conducted by the National Survey of Student Engagement in 2007 indicates that AL might be one of the few critical high-impact activities that provide experiences that enhance student learning and success. Their research indicated that student learning increased by as much as 90 percent because of AL, which has been used successfully at all levels and in classes from secondary school to college. Most pedagogical experts indicate that AL should be the main focus of what instructors ought to be doing in the classroom. It is a simple, effective, and easy teaching method or strategy based on research and common sense.

THE PROCESS

Studies by California State University in Los Angles found that professors at the university were replacing the traditional lecture environment with teaching strategies that emphasize active and cooperative learning to improve student educational experiences. They believe that these methods will enable students to internalize information presented to them in an easier and more effective manner.

According to research, there are three principal learning types integrated into AL. The first principle is entitled a, "learner-content" process where students are involved in interacting with the facts and reading material and other relevant information. The second principle is a, "learner-instructor" process in which the student's primary interaction is between the instructor and other students. The final principle is a, "learner-learner" process where the students as a whole collaborate to construct knowledge.

The U.S. Department of Education reported that learning occurs most effectively when all three types of interactive learning are utilized. In the process of AL students are given and receive projects and assignments from the instructor that require collaboration with the instructor and others and that insure that all students receive feedback and that each student develops their own point of view enabling them to apply the new acquired knowledge when needed.

Active learning consists of answering questions in class, carrying out assignments and undertakings in groups outside and inside the classroom. Interactive learning occurs when students are engaged both intellectually and emotionally and are able to connect knowledge and information found during group investigation that is provided by the instructor and other sources.

Interactive learning focuses on the process of learning in addition to acquisition of information. Feedback, contemplation, and discourse are integral components of active learning. The result of AL methods is effective instruction that connects students with strategies and techniques that have been found to teach and motivate at the same time.

Peer interaction and learning take place in and out of the classroom. The instructor/facilitator is generally present to help students understand concepts that they do not completely comprehend and require further explanation on. This back-and-forth questioning through peer interaction helps students understand new concepts while generating focus and in-depth discussions between those involved, in conjunction with the instructor.

Active instruction teaches students how to communicate effectively and team build by participating in intelligent discussions. Students have an exceptional opportunity to interact with teachers and other students as a result of these interpersonal interactions. It also allows the instructor to create a good learning atmosphere by encouragement and achieving success in an environment where students feel at ease while sharing and brainstorming together and with the instructor.

Scaffolding is an educational procedure where students establish and share common goals while providing a whole-task approach that offers available and immediate assistance when difficult situations occur. These are techniques that lead to increased learning, student participation, cooperation, and collaboration on class assignments and enable continuous monitoring and assessment by the instructor and students regarding their progress. (Scaffolding will be discussed in greater depth in the other chapters.)

Active learning takes into account the different learning styles of students such as visual and auditory and includes hands on kinesthetic learning. The great thing about AL is that the process provides instructors with a number of ways to engage secondary, college, adult, and other students. Numerous activities are available that involve and motivate students in the process of learning through active participation in their own leaning, which has become student centered.

Teachers/instructors are often confronted with students who have different backgrounds, who have different learning styles and personalities, and who have dissimilar attitudes toward study and school. Active learning helps instructor unite student differences and needs in an environment that makes it possible for students to learn cooperatively with their peers and entails meticulous planning in order to diffuse student disagreement that can often occur when engaged in new learning situations.

Although the AL instructor must follow the curriculum demands of the subject being taught, the arrangement and management of the material to be studied is left to the students' and teachers' imagination. It could include asking and answering question, explaining, clarifying, demonstrating, brainstorming, etc. Instructors use AL strategies to engage students in a hands-on approach to learning as a resource that makes learning more meaningful.

There are several methodologies that instructors can use to maximize student motivation and participation in AL because this is a type of an educational process that complements every curricular area. This method of instruction encompasses Howard Gardner's theory of multiple intelligences and is ideal for use in the major learning styles.

Active learning involves decision making that requires the development of critical-thinking and problem-solving skills that are vital to success in studies, job performance, and almost all aspects of life that requires innate creativity and inspiration. Therefore, instructors, in order to develop decision-making skills, must provide the right projects and questions that enable the listeners to develop and use rational thought and critical-thinking and problem-solving skills in order to answer questions correctly and resolve the challenges presented by the project assignments.

The objective is to supply students with compelling situations and discussion issues that require effective decision-making skills. One of the factors in developing decision-making abilities is a process called "scaffolding" in education. This process requires instructors to progressively increase the difficulty of task design and requires students to relate more with competent students and the instructor.

In summary, the active approach to learning is based on the techniques that involve students as dynamic contributors and participants in the learning process. This learning process requires the students to participate in supporting one another and allows students to develop self-confidence and improve their social skills. Therefore, the goal of active student learning is to aggressively engage students in the learning process. This is accomplished by allowing students to work together to acquire knowledge and information.

Active learning is an effective class instruction process that results in all students becoming engaged with the strategies and techniques that teach and motivate learning behavior. This style of learning includes active student participation, collaboration, and cooperation on assigned projects and activities. This AL process recognizes individual learning styles and uses ongoing student assessment. Active learning challenges students to participate directly in their own learning experiences.

Active learning enables instructors to introduce a variety of resources that actively engage students as they learn the primary educational subjects and become actively engrossed in the learning process. Learning is more comprehensive and profitable if information is dispersed in the major learning styles: visual, audio, and kinetic. Learning is also enhanced when all three of the learning styles are used to prepare students for operating in their group and eventually the entire class. These often turn out to be the activities that students most remember.

Instructor Role

An instructor/facilitator's role in active learning is to be a mentor and expediter of learning and problems solving. The objective of a facilitator is to modify and combine existing knowledge that sequentially leads to new learning. One of the major objectives of this process is to develop student learners who continue to learn throughout their life with the purpose of enhancing their ability to interact with members of society in a knowledgeable manner. This process requires all students and groups to contribute equally as expected.

Therefore, an instructor's function is to observe and direct discussions and projects in which students cooperate in a positive way by sharing responsibility for goal achievement and assigned activities. In this process, the motivation to learn depends on the learner's potential for learning and is improved through critical thinking, problem solving, and successfully experiencing challenges that occur in the environment. These positive experiences motivate the student to take part in future complicated and difficult class and group activities.

The instructor, having assumed the passive role of a facilitator of learning, helps students understand the subject matter presented and the need to develop new skills and guidelines that aid students in reaching their own conclusion. When necessary the facilitator offers a dialogue that assists students in achieving the necessary information, knowledge, and understanding of environmental experiences. This procedure is designed to support and challenge student learning and thinking processes. The end goal of a facilitator in active learning is to make it possible for students to become efficient thinkers with the instructor assuming the role of consultant.

One of the positive goals in cooperative learning is for students to learn to work as a team by asking and answering question in order to solve problems. With this, students become experts that allow them to teach others in the team/group that is having problems researching data and making rational decisions. Active-learning students should discover the principles, concepts, and facts while sharing their intuitive thinking. This collaboration and elaboration results in learners sharing information and knowledge with each team member and the class as a whole.

Active learning provides the avenue for members of a group to work with one another to reach agreement and create understanding while discovering principles, concepts, and facts, actions that might otherwise be impossible to achieve individually. Active learning is a dynamic interactive process that demands that students cooperate with each other and the instructor as a means of becoming aware of one another's point of view, which will improve relationships in all areas.

Benefits

Classroom performance will continually improve as students progress through all levels of education. One must remember that learning rests heavily on performance in previous learning situations, including home life where the attention to student learning is improved with parent participation. The benefits of active learning are numerous and the following is a list of several of them:

- Research by various studies found that students retain a minimal amount of information taught through the lecture process. On the other hand, research indicates that students involved in active learning retain about 90 percent of the data possessed.
- Active learning is a effective educational technique that engages students in their studies and increases their level of understanding because they are learning actively and not passively.
- Active learning is a result of effective instruction that connects students with strategies and techniques that have been found to teach and motivate at the same time.
- The major benefit is that learning becomes more enjoyable (fun) when students engage in new material as they learn to process information and improve knowledge through their own efforts.
- Active learning increases understanding and retention of material for students at all grade levels
- Students develop self-confidence and improve their social ability by participation in an active-learning environment

A major benefit of an AL environment is the use of various learning styles by students who, in the past, were engaged in learning by reading material and listening to a lecture. Due to AL they now learn how to acquire information and knowledge by collaborating with others to create new learning. In addition, learning is more complete and lasting than when students are engaged in simply memorizing information, which is quickly forgotten. Because of AL, students are more motivated and spend more time at the task of learning and are completely engaged in this learning procedure.

Bonwell and Edison (1991) conclude in their summation of active learning that it leads to better student attitudes and improves student thinking and writing. McKeachie (1986), in his research, found that discussion, as a form of active learning, surpassed the traditional lecture method in retention of material and increased student motivation toward further study, by improved thinking skills. Due to student involvement in AL, the potential for learning has been classified by many experts as nearly limitless.

Students, instead of being required to adjust to the learning preferences of the instructor, are now able to learn according to their needs and the styles that are most effective for them. Furthermore, because student learning is paced to meet student needs, they can quickly review previous material and focus in greater detail on learning new information.

PROBLEMS

Problems sometimes occur as a result of AL. As with any new teaching situation, additional time will be needed for both the student and the instructor to become accustomed to the process. Students working in groups can on occasion be a problem when a student does not have the social ability and the desire to participate. Controlling student behavior can be a problem when the instructor is not present, and strict discipline procedures have not been established.

Suggestions for developing classroom methods and in deciding the procedures to be used in teaching active, collaborative, and cooperative learning can also be difficult, due the lack of experience in these structured learning processes by both the teacher and student. It is of the utmost importance to keep the process simple and flexible in order to be successful in such diverse subjects as language arts, math, social studies, and the various science classes being offered in the curriculum.

The first thing that must be determined is the size of groups. Most experts recommend that the group size should be no more than four or five students. The next step is for each group to mirror the class in terms of race, gender, and ability. CHAD recommends that a four-step instructional process be instituted that begins with teaching, group study, testing, and recognition.

The instructional phase begins with presentation of information in a lecture/discussion arrangement. Students will need to know what they're going to learn and how it is going to be achieved. Throughout the group-study phase each group member works cooperatively within their respective team members while the instructor becomes a facilitator who assist with learning material and interacts with various groups when necessary. Testing takes place in two formats. The first format is individual testing and the second format is a group evaluation. In the latter format, individuals and groups are given recognition based on evaluation scores as a class, group, and class membership.

Multimedia

Today educators have available many additional resources that enhance learning. Research indicates that active-learning techniques and approaches to learning can be used at any grade level and subject. In addition, a multimedia learning system can embrace an assortment of technologies that includes PowerPoint, whiteboards, computers, and the Internet to assist the acquisition of knowledge. Videos are often used to encourage students and to enhance the transmission of the content being studied.

Active learning encourages the use of multimedia in this learning process. It is believed by many experts in education that multimedia can aid students with different learning styles. Almost any educational activity can become active by designing learning activities that increase student curiosity. Video and interactive computer learning will help involve students in additional pedagogical experiences. Instructors today are able to enhance learning with a wide range of media resources such as visual data that conveys ideas and content more easily than verbal descriptions, which is an important learning device in classroom enhancement.

Research found that learning is improved when charts, diagrams, and other visual presentations are used. Videos and other visuals are easier for students to absorb and increase engagement in the content being presented. Studies in these active interactions showed that students and teachers can use multimedia to show what they should know and as a means of transmitting course content. Additional information regarding active learning, in addition to decision making, analytical reasoning, problem solving, and critical-thinking skills and strategies, can be found in appendix D.

Active learning is a method of instruction that actively engages students in the learning process. Simply put, active learning requires students to meaningfully learn from activities and to think about what they are trying to accomplish.

Chapter Four

Cooperative Learning

Cooperative learning (COL) is an instructional form of team/group effort in which students pursue common goals while being assessed individually and as a team. This process incorporates individual interaction and accountability, mutual interdependence, face-to-face interpersonal skills, and regular self and group assessments of how the team/groups have functioned.

The following is a brief summation of research and why scientists concluded that cooperative learning is one of the major aspects of learning and an effective teaching methodology. Cooperative learning is based on the premise that cooperation is more effective than competition among students for producing positive learning outcomes. The following are two brief definitions of cooperative learning: 1) the act of working in compliance with others, 2) association with others for the mutual benefit of a common cause where the objective is to make things easier and improve understanding.

Cooperative learning, which was established prior to World War II by several social theorists, is a specific kind of collaborative learning, in which students learn by participating in small peer groups to achieve prearranged structured endeavors. They are individually accountable for their own performance and the efforts of the group as a whole.

Cooperative groups work face-to-face in numbers of four or five while working as teams in order to share their strengths and also to enhance their weaker skills. In their groups, students develop interpersonal skills while learning to deal with conflicts, and are guided by clear objectives. Students engage in numerous activities that improve their understanding of the subject being studied.

Cooperative learning is also an educational approach to learning that organizes academic and social experiences into classroom activities. Cooperative learning is defined from an educational viewpoint as a structured form of group work in which students engage in common goals while being evaluated individually and as a group. Cooperative learning is the interaction of replacing and intermixing individual thoughts and ideas. Its core is based on the premise that student cooperation in learning activities is more effective than student competition in generating constructive learning experiences and outcomes.

In addition, research shows that cooperation also promotes interpersonal relationships, enhances social support, and improves self-esteem. Research also indicates that there are three things necessary for groups to accomplish in order to create an environment in which COL can take place. First, students need to be challenged in a secure environment that provides a sense of safety. Second, small groups need to be established in which all participants can and must contribute and, third, a clear definition must be given regarding the task that students work on together.

Slavin in his study of the research found the following concepts that are required for effective COL:

- Students are evaluated both as a group and individually.
- Success of the group is not based only on individual performance but by all team members assisting each other in achieving group learning goals.
- Each student's individual performance is expected to excel, thereby challenging other members to do their best, as a group and individually, in order to contribute to group knowledge.

Andrew Dahley, defined COL as a process where students work with their peers to accomplish shared or common goals. Each student's goals are achieved through interdependence by the entire group, instead of working independently. Thus, individual members are held accountable for the outcome of the group's shared goal or goals.

Wikipedia.com defines COL as an academic and social learning approach to organizing classroom activities that has been described as structural, positive, and interdependent. It's a process where students learn in groups to complete assignments collectively to achieve their academic goals, unlike individual leaning, which leads to competition among students.

Instead, students in COL share resources and skills by asking other students for information, evaluating each other's ideas, and monitoring other members' work. In addition, the teacher's role becomes one of providing information as a facilitator of knowledge and student learning in which all students succeed when the group is successful.

Panitz's studies concluded that COL was effective in developing interpersonal skills and teamwork among students. His research concluded that it is sensible to assume that the practice of interpersonal skills, when coupled with explicit instruction in social skills, would be more effective than traditional learning.

According to Johnson, Johnson, and Smith there are five details in COL that include: 1) individual and group accountability, 2) mutual interdependence, 3) face-to-face interaction, 4) development of interpersonal skills, and 5) regular individual and group evaluations. They determined that the main objective of COL is that, instead of students competing, they act together to promote learning.

Prince's conclusions, based on empirical evidence, state that the central premise of COL is that it is more effective than competition for promoting a wide range of learning outcomes. These results included enhanced academic achievement and improvement in the attitudes displayed by students. In conclusion, COL provides a natural environment that enhances interpersonal skills. However, it differs from most group work in that it is considered a structured positive interdependence in which competitive individual learning is replaced with cooperative student learning.

Students learn to work cooperatively as a team by capitalizing on each other's resources and skills. Learning is improved when students share individual information, evaluate each other's ideas and monitor their team's work. The instructor's role in COL is that of a facilitator of information/ knowledge that creates student learning. Therefore, instead of the learner attempting to accomplish success on their own they work as a team in which all members succeed together. The learning objective of COL discussions are for students to work to seek answers to questions in which each group member has different questions that are developed to increase cognitive ability, thus allowing students to progress and meet their learning objectives.

The following are factors that experts found to be important in developing small groups or teams:

- Goals are clearly identified and used as a guide to learning.
- Respect is given to every member of the team.
- Projects and questions provide interest and challenge to individual students as well as to team/group.
- Diversity is accepted and all contributions are valued.
- Students learn the skills for resolving conflicts.
- Each member draws upon their past experience and knowledge.
- Research tools such as the Internet can be made available.

Ross and Smyth (1995), in addition to several other researchers, have described cooperative learning as intellectually demanding, creative and open-ended and requiring higher levels of thinking skills. They outlined several essential elements that are required for success in corporation of cooperative learning in the classroom. These components are listed below:

- **Positive interdependence,** which states that students must fully participate in team efforts and are responsible for their learning when students have a specific goal or goals to achieve. To achieve their goals, students must support, and have support from, other members on the team in learning the material being studied. In addition they will be assessed by individual and group evaluations or reviews regarding the material being studied and their contribution to the group.
- **Promote face-to-face interaction,** which requires each group member to be responsible for each other's success in understanding and completion of assignments. In that most students have not developed many interpersonal skills, they must be taught basic leadership, decision making, trust building, and communication skills. Otherwise, when conflict arises over differences of opinion among team members, problems can arise that causes disunity and may be disruptive to individual understanding and, most importantly, create disagreement among group/team members that affects overall performance.
- **Individual and group accountability** stipulates that individual members of a team are required to contribute significantly in order to achieve their common group goals. Individual contribution is evaluated by individual evaluation scores that require the completion of a group project. Individual accountability requires each student to demonstrate a high level of knowledge and accountability for learning, while "social loafing" must be eliminated.
- **Social skills education** requires the instructor to teach and students to learn social skills that include communication, interpersonal, and group skills, in addition to the skills of leadership, decision making, and trust building, which includes conflict management.
- **Group processing** includes the assessment of individual and group performance and goal achievement. The group process allows the instructor to achieve a better understanding of students within the groups and the ability to correct undesirable individual and group behavior.

When instructors and students design the cooperative tasks to be learned, a grading/reward system must also be developed that evaluates individual accountability and responsibilities. Once this has been completed, students can be placed in teams. The entire team is presented with the lesson to be achieved and each team member is given individual or group tasks to accomplish in order to complete the group's project/s. Once the lessons are completed each student is evaluated and graded on the team and individual performance.

- Student evaluations are taken individually and graded on individual and team performance in order to encourage each group to work as a team to improve overall performance, as a means of achieving group goal success.
- Each individual student must know exactly what their responsibilities are and be held accountable to the group for performance completion.
- Furthermore, all group members must be involved in order to complete group tasks. This can only occur if each member assumes responsibility and accountability to achieve the task or tasks assigned and complete their assignments in a timely fashion.
- Once the task has been completed, the group collaborates to reach a conclusion to the challenges, questions, or problems that were their learning objectives. Cognitive ability will improve due to the differentiated results of each participants contribution to objective achievement (Tsay 2010).

TYPES OF COOPERATIVE LEARNING

Research indicates that cooperative learning is of two types: formal and informal. In formal cooperative learning, educators must develop a process that is structured, facilitated, and monitored. The objective of this process is to achieve group goals and assigned tasks in groups that can vary from two to six students. In group presentations and discussions, learning strategies involve groups in critical thinking, problem solving, decision making, or laboratory or experiment assignments that are followed by peer reviews.

Formal cooperative learning peer groups generally stay together for an extensive period of time, which enables them to contribute to one another's knowledge and mastery of the topic on a regular basis. This occurs when student groups discuss material, encourage each other, and support individual and group academic and personal success. Informal COL encompasses group learning with passive instruction. The results of this procedure allow students to process, consolidate, and retain more learned information. These groups are temporary and can change from lesson to lesson.

If discussions are the main objective of a group assignment, they are generally composed of four parts that include: 1) formulating responses to question presented by the instructor, 2) sharing responses to questions asked by a group participant, 3) listening to a team member's response to questions, or 4) creating new well-thought-out and well-developed answers to the questions being discussed. The long-term result of effective group learning establishes caring and supportive peer group relationships which will in turn motivate and strengthen student commitment to the group's education, while making students accountable for helping educate their peers.

BENEFITS OF COOPERATIVE LEARNING

The question often asked about cooperative learning is, "Does it really work?" The answer is that the vast majority of studies regarding COL have shown this learning process to be more effective than non-cooperative-learning instruction in motivating students and producing positive social outcomes. Research also shows that students learn more by doing something and getting immediate feedback than by listening and watching someone tell them what they should learn and know. This occurs because students take responsibility for their own group learning by taking advantage of these learning opportunities.

Additional research overwhelmingly confirms that COL increases school and class satisfaction, school attendance, motivation, independence, and personal and social development in those students who fully participated in group activities and cooperated with their other group members (Brady and Tsay 2010). Research by Keller and Steinhorst (1995), who examined different learning approaches at college and university levels, found positive results from cooperative learning. Hinde and Kovac (2001) report that test scores were higher in cooperative and active learning classes than in traditional classes.

John Dewey, a well-respected education theorist, insisted that it was important that students cultivate knowledge and social skills in order to develop abilities that could be used outside of the classroom and in a democratic society. His theory described learners as recipients of knowledge obtained from discussing information and answers questions in groups and being actively engaged in the learning process as a group, instead of being passive individual receivers of knowledge and information

Slavin's study in 1994 and other studies found that cooperative learning produced bigger increases in some aspects of self-esteem than non-cooperative methods. These studies also found that cooperative learning groups had a higher regard for their group members and wanted to come to school more than other students did. These and other findings also concluded:

- Student displays increased academic achievement.
- COL methods were equally efficient for all ability levels.
- COL is effective for all ethnic groups in that it enhances student social ability.
- It enhanced student self-esteem and self-concept.
- It encouraged learning goals in place of performance goals.
- Cooperative groups were easier to supervise than individual students.
- Cooperation makes possible instant feedback to students and teacher.
- It encourages students to seek help and accept peer assistance.

- It promotes meta-cognition, the ability of students to recognize and analyze learning.
- It improves student ability to recall text content for discussions.

Slavin (2010) in his further research concluded that COL produced greater student learning and achievement than traditional learning methodologies. Slavin found that 63 percent of the students analyzed increased their class achievement. His studies showed that in cooperative teams, all members achieved success. He also found that low-achieving students tried harder when teamed with students who had higher achievement levels. He also concluded that there were social benefits in that students will take risks when praised for their contribution to the group. Social skills are developed in students with different cultural backgrounds, attitudes, and personalities: COL was effective for all ethnic groups.

Taman's research (1996) indicates that cooperative learning infuses social skills training into the academic curriculum. Heterogeneous learning groups were found to be effective in promoting student learning when students had to deal with and communicate with others to solve conflicts that arise in group interaction. In addition there appear to be some economic benefits in COL in that fewer materials are needed due to mutual sharing. In sharing teaching materials, students learn to value limited resource and time on task.

Johnson and Johnson's research (1989–1995) found that cooperative learning produced higher levels of performance in the following factors, compared to competitive and individual learning:

- Increase in higher levels of reasoning
- Learners actively participate more in class
- Improvements in initiating new ideas and solutions
- Greater transfer of learning between situations
- Promotes positive attitudes
- Student learning experiences are enhanced
- Consistency, built student self-esteem and self-efficacy
- Group work provided a greater chance of success for some students
- Accommodates differences in learning styles: kinesthetic-auditory-visual
- Students learn important life skills by working together and collaborating their ideas
- Students benefit from working as a team to accomplish tasks that would otherwise have been very difficult.
- Resulted in deeper understanding of content leading to an overall increase in grades, leading to higher levels of self-effacy and esteem, while improving motivation to complete the activities encountered
- Increased activity and constructive involvement in content and students were more willing to take ownership of their own learning

- Achieved the ability to resolve group conflicts quicker and improved teamwork skills
- Students became more devoted in their own learning

D. Johnson, R. Johnson, and Kari Smith found that test scores of cooperative-learning students were two-thirds of a standard deviation higher than students in competitive and individual classes. Studies by Johnson and Slavin found that the factors most responsible for learning gains are group goals and individual accountability, which are a major aspect of cooperative learning. Another factor responsible for student improvement was motivation, which led to extra time on task and the desire to work harder in achieving goals.

David and Roger Johnson in 1975 found that cooperative learning promoted mutual liking, better communication, high acceptance, support, and an increase in a variety of thinking abilities among individual students. They also concluded that there was less interactive competition and greater trust among individuals in the group. In their 1986 research they concluded that COL Increased higher reasoning levels while improving the origination of new ideas and solutions to problems.

It becomes obvious when reviewing the research that COL discussions enable students to process, consolidate, and retain more information as a result of discussions in which students respond to questions asked by the instructor, sharing responses to the questions of other students, and listening to their responses.

It was concluded that this learning process enables students to consolidate and retain more learned information.

These investigations further showed tremendous achievement outcomes, causing researchers to conclude that cooperative learning also contributed to improvement in problem solving. It was concluded by Qin, Johnson, and Johnson that COL students of all ages, from elementary to college, outscored students who worked in a competitive environment.

One of the great contributions of COL is the equality of opportunity for achieving success in heterogeneous groups. Most studies indicate students in cooperative groups with classmates of different races, ethnic groups, social classes, and mental abilities were more likely to be friends. They also concluded that cooperative skills learned were transferred successfully to out-of-school situations.

For COL to be effective, it is important that all avenues of learning be opened to assure that all students have the opportunity to contribute to their group. In addition to achievement outcomes, research concluded that COL had a tremendous impact on problem-solving ability, compared to competitive learning among students.

These studies also concluded that cooperative-learning students were more motivated to learn because of increased self-esteem. In addition, these studies concluded that educating through small interactive groups builds a more robust knowledge structure and student motivation. The anticipation of immediate feedback from reactions by their peers and instructors was a very strong motivator. In most instances students want the immediate feedback produced by group work in order to better understand their progress.

COOPERATIVE LEARNING LIMITATIONS

Although there are tremendous amounts of positive research regarding COL there is also some, but limited, research regarding its limitations. Sharan (2006) indicates that the major limitations of COL were that this learning process is constantly changing, thus confusing instructors, which may lead to a lack of a complete understanding of the COL process. In addition, teachers who implement COL are challenged by students who resist involvement in the program because slower teammates or those who are less competent will produce less work due to their perceived competition among peers. It's also possible that students lacking in self-confidence feel that they will be ignored or degraded by their team.

A major problem with group learning is competition between groups. Competition serves a good purpose; however, it is rarely used effectively. However, it can be used efficiently to motivate performance, if not used too often and done in the absence of norm-related grading procedures. Instructors often have problems with COL due to unfamiliarity with the process, fear of losing control in the classroom, fear that procedures are too time consuming, and fear that they lacked ability to control content being covered.

For some instructors, it is important to show their expertise in a subject area, which may hinder an instructor's desire to use COL in the classroom (ego). In addition, the instructor may be faced with questions that they cannot answer, owing to the student's ability to research in areas unfamiliar to the instructor. This can be overcome by the instructor using their position as a facilitator of knowledge rather than as a dispenser of information. Therefore, some form of self-management must be established before grouping and constantly reinforcing a group's progress.

Problems associated with cooperative learning tend to be due to vague objectives, lack of direct curriculum teaching by the instructor, and the lack of critical thinking endeavors on the part of the student. Occasionally, some students may not be getting the guidance for effective learning, due to the time required in small group learning, while instructors may not assign tasks that demand higher levels of thinking due the additional time requirements. Students working in small groups generally escalate the noise level within the classroom that can often be distracting for the teacher and other classmates.

WHY DOES COOPERATIVE LEARNING WORK?

The question often asked about cooperative learning is, Does it really work? The answer is that you have seen that the vast majority of studies regarding COL show COL as being more effective than non-cooperative-learning instruction in motivating students and producing positive social outcomes. Studies indicate that cooperative learning produced bigger increases in some aspects of self-esteem than did non-cooperative methods and that cooperative learning groups had a higher regard for their group members and wanted to come to school more than did non-cooperative-learning students. Cooperative learners consistently produced higher self-efficacy scores than competitive and individual learners.

Researchers, in trying to clarify why cooperative learning is so successful in improving student performance, have cited the following reasons:

- Motivation: Due to positive interdependence, students are highly motivated, which leads to achievement-orientated behaviors such as trying hard, regular class attendance, praising the efforts of others, and helping group members. Meanwhile, COL learning is seen as a responsible and worthwhile activity as a result of group success and cooperative effort.
- Cognitive Improvement: Vygotsky found that COL promotes cognitive growth by modeling more advanced ways of thinking.
- Cognitive Elaboration: New information indicates that learning is restructured by relating it to existing knowledge, making it easier to recall from memory. Elaboration is based on the fact that if you can't tell someone what you know, you don't know it.

THE INSTRUCTOR'S ROLE

In cooperative learning the instructor's role is very important as a facilitator who controls the learning process. Thus, it becomes very important to establish a COL learning environment, in which the teacher, to be effective, assumes the role of a facilitator of learning. As a facilitator he or she must know the characteristics of each student and group. Grouping of students is often a difficult process, and each group must be chosen with great care and understanding. Additional factors that the facilitators must consider are the difference in learning styles, cultural background, personalities, and the gender and ethnic makeup of each group.

Establishing the proper environment for COL would be for the instructor to encourage students to construct their own group management contract in which they set their own goals and rules of conduct. This process should help students work together with more responsibility and more cooperatively by setting standards for their group.

Having devoted a great deal of time to preparing COL lessons, the facilitator then assumes a background role. Due to time limitations, the textbook is used as one of the instructional supplements. Thus, the instructor must develop a student handbook that contains an instructional syllabus and additional group activities needed to complete the course. The instructor now has initiated a new process for learning and has created the educational materials needed to teach the entire curriculum.

After the lessons to be learned have been implemented, the facilitator becomes somewhat of a spectator as he or she watches students teach themselves as well as teaching each other. Cooperative lessons allow students to learn from their peers and become less dependent on the facilitator for assistance. The instructor must train students in conflict resolution, cultural diversity, group management, and respect for others. Often, the teacher becomes a learner and the learners sometime become teachers.

Evaluations

Because students work together on group assignments, it can turn out to be a difficult process to assess individual and group improvement. Evaluations can take place and be determined as a team and/or individually. Due to the tremendous number of COL assessment techniques obtainable, they will not be discussed in great detail in this chapter but will be discussed with the other learning theories.

GROUP/TEAM PROCESS

The major factor in the group process is deciding how groups are to be formed in order for students to work together to achieve maximum performance. Research consensus indicates that groups should consist of no more than four to five students. Once the number of members has been determined, the composition of each group must be decided. The factors that need to be established are gender, race, intellect, and the students' willingness to participate.

Advanced students must understand that part of their responsibilities in COL learning is to guide lower skilled students, while lower level students must understand they are responsible for group work and participation with advanced students. The key is that everybody participates in learning and shares in the achievements of the group. Group assessment is a process of how a group or individual students are functioning in order to achieve their goals and complete assignments.

Some form of assessment must be used to determine if improvement is occurring and how students are working together to achieve group goals and the success of individual learning. By reviewing group behavior and achievement, the students and the facilitator can discuss specific needs or problems and how to solve these problems individually, responsibly, and with accountability.

Proper behavior must be identified so that students understand their responsibilities and obligations and that each student will be held accountable for individual and group performance. Occasionally group performance should be assessed for its effectiveness and areas that need improvement. In order to assess student achievement, two characteristics must exist. The first area to be considered is each student working to achieve group goals and recognition. In the construct of COL, student responsibility and accountability must recognize that tasks and evaluations will include individual as well as group achievement.

The second factor is individual learning, which requires positive interdependence to be present among students who are attempting to achieve their goals and complete their responsibilities. Groups must be given an opportunity to express their opinions about the problems and the benefits of the group-learning process and the ability to correct undesired behavior, in additions to celebrating their success as a group.

Assessing performance requires that all groups encompass the following factors:

- **Positive interdependence** takes place when students have a specific goal or goals to accomplish. To achieve positive interdependence, students must support the group process in order to receive support from other members in the group while learning the materials being studied. Also, they will be assessed by individual and group exams or reviews regarding the material being studied, in addition to their contribution to the group.
- **Pro-motive interaction** is necessary due to the existence of positive interdependence in that students must be knowledgeable in how to help other students overcome problems that occur, in order to complete assigned projects. This process includes peer tutoring, temporary assistance, and exchanges of information. In addition, students will challenge one another's reason for providing feedback and encouragement to keep the group motivated toward completing the required project and assignments.
- **Individual accountability** stipulates that all individual members of a group are required to contribute significantly in order to achieve the group's goals. Individual contributions are evaluated by individual test scores based on the requirements for completion of a group project.
- **Interpersonal skills**: In order for a group to survive, members must understand how to communicate in face-to-face interactions. Since most

students may not have developed many interpersonal skills, they must be taught basic leadership, decision making, trust building, and communication skills. Therefore, when conflict arises over differences of opinion, it can disrupt group cohesion: solutions for group differences can be achieved.

KEY IDEAS TO REMEMBER

Cooperative learning is based on the fact that working together in small heterogeneous groups, (four to five students), will most likely lead to the ability to master various aspects of new tasks and assignments. Thanks to the success achieved when working as a group, students become more motivated to learn because they know they will accumulate new knowledge. Furthermore, stronger interpersonal relationships will be forged that could not be achieved alone. For the team's effort to be judged successful, each member of the group must perform at a certain level.

The end results are that equal opportunities for success are made available to students of all capability levels. The ability to be a factor in a team's success requires each member to contribute in achieving group accomplishments and team success. Slavin (1995) found that cooperative learning produced bigger increases in some aspects of self-esteem than non-cooperative methods. He also found that cooperative learning groups had a higher regard for their group members and wanted to come to school more than did other students.

Johnson and Johnson, in their studies, also found that COL consistently produced higher self-efficacy scores than competitive and individual situations. Because of the role played by COL in enhancing the education of all students, it should be infused into all subjects being taught. For example COL is the key to successful discussions in group work. In addition, students work together to learn important educational and life skills by collaborating in their ideas with other students.

Tayman's (1996) research indicates that COL "Infuses social skill training into the academic curriculum," while Hodne (1997) stated that the ideal classroom would place students in groups that coordinate their roles and resources, as well as celebrating their achievements. Research indicates that COL is very important in establishing the appropriate learning environment and can only be achieved by students who institute a classroom management contract in which they set their own rules of conduct. This process would encourage the students to work cooperatively as a group in addition to being more responsible for their conduct and behavior, both individually and as a group and as a class.

Richard Felder and Rebecca asked the question, "How do I get teams off to a good start?" Most students do not possess the knowledge and have not developed their capability to function effectively on a student team. Therefore, the facilitator must work to establish a learning environment that supports effective student teams. Many of the challenges that occur when using student teams can most effectively be addressed at the beginning of the course.

This is when student teams can identify potential concerns, including possible leader and participant issues, while developing norms of behavior through which these concerns can be addressed. In addition the facilitator can put forth the policies for addressing problems that may occur downstream and can lay out the evaluation policies that will address grading team assignments. Assessment and group development and other cooperative factors can be found in chapter 9 and appendix D.

Chapter Five

Collaborative Learning

Cooperative learning (COL): refers to any instructional method that places students in groups that work toward common goals that emphasize student interaction to solve problems. Collaborative learning is a teaching procedure that is similar to the teaching methods found in other theories and educational concepts discussed in this manuscript. Collaborative learning (COLL) consists of any instructional approach in which students engage in small groups and work together to achieve common goals, while being assessed on individual and team bases. Therefore, the core components of COLL are based on students learning through interacting rather than learning in the traditional method.

Collaborative learning consists of learning situations comprised of two-plus individuals where they attempt to learn things by working together to solve problems and other assignments proposed by the instructor. The following are several definitions of collaborative learning:

- to work jointly with others in an intellectual endeavor;
- to cooperate with or are willing to participate with others;
- to cooperate with others or someone not immediately connected to them
- a process in which two or more students participate together to realize shared goals.

Collaborative learning differs from individual learning in that members of the class work in groups or teams cooperatively to capitalize on the combined resources of each member's skills and knowledge and by asking questions and evaluating each other's information and ideas. This procedure of learning is based on the premise that knowledge is created when students actively interact to share experience with other students in a group. In this method learners create and share ideas in a learning environment.

It is in a COLL atmosphere that students become engaged in common activities in which each member depends on and is accountable to other students in the group. Group discussions in COLL could include conversation, statistical discourse, and analysis of the topic being studied, and so on.

RESEARCH

Vygotsky's view and research concluded that COLL is based on the idea that there exists an inherent social nature of learning found in all students. This social nature involves a joint intellectual effort by learners as a group/team and in conjunction with the instructor to work together in their search for understanding, solving problems, comprehending meaning, or producing a product. Collaborative learning takes place when individual students become actively engaged with team members and produce learning as a result of their specific and implied efforts.

Simply put, COLL is a process where a group/team of students learns together and in union with an instructor/facilitator who supervises and provides feedback about each team's and individual student's effort regarding their work and progress. Gerlach (1994) concluded that student learning takes place best in natural social events where the participants talk among themselves. It is through this deliberation that learning takes place. Smith and MacGregor (1992) developed the following assumptions concerning collaborative learning.

They concluded:

1. COLL is an active learning process that incorporates information and associates this new knowledge with prior knowledge. This is accomplished by making students responsible for learning.
2. COLL allows students to engage with their peers as a process of producing information while increasing knowledge, instead of memorizing and reiterating it to the instructor and/or other students.
3. Benefits are realized when students are exposed to diverse points of view brought forth by people of dissimilar backgrounds.
4. During intellectual discussion and social environments, learners design a framework and are able to apply meaning to their discourse. In these situations students engage in the opportunity to carry on discussions with their peers, exchange diverse beliefs, present and defend their ideas, and question the conceptual ideas of other learners.

5. These groups employ activities that help students achieve a relaxing feeling with each other by accepting a diversity of ideas and by instituting tolerance in the classroom among learning groups.

Research conducted by Johnson, Johnson, and Smith (1989) found that COLL had greater learning benefits and outcomes when COLL students were compared to students doing individual tasks. Springer's research found a consistent improvement in student grades and longer retention of information as a result of participating in COLL programs when compared with traditional learning. In collaborative learning, student labor collectively in small groups to actively achieve understanding and knowledge in regard to designated goals.

Collaborative learning improves learning by establishing roles and mediating interactions while constructing flexibility in dialogue and group activities. Johnson and Johnson largely centered their assessment of COLL instructional procedures based on the social interdependence theory of group development. They justified this position by indicating that when individuals take action they have three procedures that may affect the actions of others. Their efforts can support the achievement of other students, which may or may not hinder their success

Therefore, they concluded that individuals in a working group may: 1) work together in a cooperative effort as a group to achieve shared learning goals; 2) compete against other group members in attempting to attain a goal or goals that only one or a few can attain; 3) work individually to accomplish goals that are unrelated to group goals.

Johnson and Johnson (1998), in their review of educational research, indicate that cooperative efforts, when compared with competitive and individual attempts, in general, created higher levels of achievement and superior productivity. In addition, collaborative learning groups were socially more caring, supportive, and committed to relationships and achieved greater psychological health, social competence, and self-esteem.

Collaborative learning, if planned properly, improves student learning more than individual learning. On the other hand, a poorly designed collaborative learning curriculum will not promote established learning goals effectively or efficiently. COLL formats promote a number of interactive processes that are conducive to learning success.

THE PROCESS

Collaborative learning is said to encompass all approaches to learning. Experts in COLL explain that the emphasis of the core element is based on student interaction rather than individual learning. Johnson, Johnson, and

Smith (1991) concluded that a learning exercise only qualifies as COLL if the following are present:

1. Students working together and asking and answering questions while relying on each other. When the group takes part in answering difficult questions and solving challenging problems and situations, students are able to talk and get to know each other during class, which will carry over outside of the classroom.
2. Collaborative learning redefines traditional student associations in the classroom and group settings, which has a constructive effect on student learning.
3. Based on positive interdependence and individual accountability, group members depend on each other to complete assignments that achieve their assigned goals. All students in a group are held accountable for doing their share of work in order to achieve mastery of all the material learned.
4. Although some groups may work individually, others complete activities interactively, which provides student groups with feedback that challenge each member's supposition and analysis while encouraging other group participants with whom they agree.
5. Collaborative development creates and encourages trust building, decision making, leadership, and communication as well as how to handle conflicting situations.
6. In order to function efficiently and effectively, student groups are required to set goals, periodically assess team attainment, and produce methods that improve their learning achievement.

LEARNING OBJECTIVES

Collaborative learning also develops a quicker assessment of a certain amount of resource material and creates the capacity to apply and share knowledge and principles that increase student understanding of complex concepts, while improving the ability to solve problems. This leads to enhanced creativity and understanding of different prospective, improves management of prejudice and bias, increases diversity and valuing that develops positive attitudes toward learning, and fosters meta-cognition in that students are involved in recognition and analysis of how to learn.

Collaborative learning scholars and professionals tend to come from the humanities and social sciences. Their work often explores theoretical, political, and philosophical issues such as the nature of comprehension as a social construction and the role of authority in the classroom. Collaborative learning practitioners are inclined to assume that students will be responsible participants who already use their social skills in undertaking and completing tasks. Therefore, students receive less instruction in group skills and roles, while performing in less structured situations. Therefore, when a group member fails to do his or her part; the consequences will be suffered by the whole group.

BENEFITS OF COLLABORATIVE LEARNING

Research analysis shows that collaboration enhances academic achievement, student attitudes, and knowledge retention. Proponents of COLL claim that the active exchange of ideas in small groups increases interest in learning, promotes critical thinking, and achieves higher levels of thought and students retain information longer than individual learners. This learning process develops a quicker assessment of a certain quantity of resource material by creating the ability to apply and share knowledge principles and increases understanding of complex concepts while improving problem-solving ability.

Student involved in COLL show increases in achievement that promote interpersonal relationships, improve social support, and foster self-esteem. This process leads to improved creativity and the understanding of different prospective and improves behavior management while increasing positive attitudes toward learning in addition to improving self-esteem. There are many benefits achieved when students are allowed to work and complete assignments together in that this enables students to take on the teacher's role as dispenser of information.

An analysis of COLL indicates that collaboration enhanced academic achievement, student attitudes toward learning, and retention of pertinent information and knowledge. A proponent of COLL claims that the active exchange of ideas in small groups, in addition to increasing student interest in learning, also promotes critical thinking, higher levels of thought and retention of information longer than individual learning, while enhancing student satisfaction with the learning experience that promotes positive attitudes toward the subject matter being studied. Research indicates that COLL:

- develops social interaction and oral communication skills;
- enhances self-management skills;
- uses a team approach to problem solving while maintaining individual accountability;
- encourages student responsibility for learning that involves students in developing curriculum and class procedures;
- stimulates critical thinking by helping students clarify ideas through discussion and debate

- establishes an atmosphere of cooperation;
- promotes learning goals in place of performance goals due to interaction and interdependence among groups;
- promotes students' developing responsibility for one another;
- encourages alternate student assessment of techniques, which significantly reduces assessment and evaluation anxiety;
- encourages diversity by group interaction;
- encourages development of assessment techniques that are not competitive
- provides for immediate feedback.

COLLABORATIVE HANDICAPS

Research indicates that both the instructor and students encounter challenges that accompany collaborative learning situations. Instructors, especially at first, may feel that there is never enough:

- time to develop activities;
- time to teach group dynamics;
- time to implement collaborative learning activities
- time in class for students to work on small group projects.

Furthermore, some educators feel it could be intimidating when attempting to put into practice new collaborative lessons because of the concern that the "experimental" activity may not work smoothly when assigned for the first time. Then there's the grading issue: how are group projects to be evaluated? The following is an additional list of factors that research indicates may hinder the establishment of COLL:

- Students come to class with varying degrees of interpersonal and academic skills.
- Students will need to understand how group participation affects their grades.
- Collaborative learning may make introverted students apprehensive because it requires them to communicate verbally.
- Students cannot remain passive or disengaged.
- Students who are academically competitive and self-motivated may resent collaborative learning, at first, because of the fear that they will do most of the work while other members of their group will simply not complete their own assignments.
- Instructors will need to decide how to grade collaborative activities equitably.

As an instructor, one way to begin overcoming these hurdles is to ask experienced colleagues to serve as "collaborative learning mentors" by finding out what has worked for them. Ask them how they located or created resources for use in collaborative settings, and observe them in their classroom using collaborative strategies.

PREPARING STUDENTS FOR GROUP WORK

An understanding of the following factors will enable educators to develop successful, efficient, and proficient COLL groups. Each factor is based on the research found in scientific publications and on the Internet regarding COLL group development. Additional information can be found in appendix D.

The Teacher's Role

Experts indicate that, for some reason, there is very little research on the important topic of the teacher's role in group learning. The following information will enable the instructor to better understand their role as facilitators in COLL. Before dividing students and assigning them to collaborative groups, instructors must train students in the skills required to perform group assignments efficiently, effectively, and productively. By informing students with knowledge and understanding of the way this process works, instructors can teach student teams how to build exercises that encourages mutual respect and caring among student groups/teams.

In this process, the teacher prepares students by providing group standards for students to use as a guideline regarding how to function proficiently in a group setting. The information needed is usually posted in the classroom as a visible reminder to students of the importance of treating each other with respect and listening open-mindedly to other opinions that allow students to engage in positive interactions.

Some research regarding the facilitator's role in COLL presents varied proposals regarding their involvement in group work. Most experts agree that the instructor needs to be listening attentively to what students say in order to evaluate the quality of their interactions. On the other hand, there are researchers who believe that instructors must be active by getting involved frequently to assist groups when needed. However, others believe that instructors should actively walk around and listen carefully but should only interact with the groups on a minimal basis.

Group/Team Size and Composition

In researching the conditions for effective collaborative learning, one of the things that stands out the most is the need to determine group composition. Group composition can be defined by several variables that include age, ethnic makeup of participants, the size of each group, and the differences in the educational development level between group members.

In making decisions on the number of members in each group, it should be understood that small groups seem to work better than large groups. When considering group size, consideration must be given to differences in mutual regulation, social mixture, and shared cognitive load that can only occur in groups with a few participants and where instructors take care to see that no learner is left out of any interaction.

In determining who the group participants will be, consideration must be given to the educational level of students in each group. The most studied variable of group participation is the perception students possess about other members in the group. These differences can be age, intelligence, level of development, previous school performance, personality, ethnic background and, on occasion, appearance. Although studies show that in order to trigger group interaction about the subject being studied, there should be some differences in viewpoints between participants.

Therefore, these differences must be within the boundaries of mutual interest, respect, and intelligence. In general, if left to their own devices, students without supervision have natural tendencies to congregate with others who are similar to them or whom they know. The ideal group size varies according to the task. Grouping into pairs has been shown to be effective in many implementations of collaborative learning. Although most programs use larger groups, they are typically no larger than six students to a group.

More importantly, groups of four to five appear to provide the best number when working on complicated tasks. This is because groups need to interact frequently, which is best accomplished with groups of six or fewer. Lander's study in 1995 found that small groups were easier to supervise and evaluate. The composition of groups should be heterogeneous and composed of students who differ in gender, ability, and diverse ethnic backgrounds and composed of students who are comparable to each other in these features.

However, a single ideal type of group composition has not been identified by researchers. With this in mind, diverse minority groups should not be allowed to work together as a group. A good alternative would be to find a means of assigning groups to make available flexible grouping so that students from diverse groups can be reorganized when needed. Grouping could also be based on student interests, on those who need additional work on a specific skill, or on diversity of background knowledge pertinent to the assigned task.

Collaborative learning has the capability of achieving highly effective approaches to instruction. However, instructors must realize COLL is not always going to be effective in the procedures commonly used by instructors. It is evident that only those methods that promote a productive COLL group process are those that provide the support required by students who are effective and efficient when taking part in difficult assignments. Nelson-LeGall (1992) stated that COLL encourages students to seek help and be willing to accept assistance for their peers.

There are, however, a number of formats that promote an interactive course of group action that are beneficial to learning. The first of these processes is engagement. When groups are engaged and interested in the task at hand they are less likely to develop off-task behaviors such as "social loafing." David and Roger Johnson (1991) have called attention to the importance of positive interdependence. They suggested that this process can only occur when students complete a task by working together. Barron (2003) stated that effective positive interdependence is required and is most likely to occur when joint attention is directed to the tasks at hand.

This means that all students who are focused on a similar undertaking, often literally looking at the same data, are involved in discussions about a common topic. In order to reduce students working individually, the instructor must monitor discussions and hold meetings that require individual and group progress reports. This will eliminate student concerns about group members who fail to do their fair share. This can also be achieved by grading student performance individually, as a group, and by peer-on-peer evaluation. Collaborative groups/teams must be kept together until team building is achieved and they are working effectively to complete the required assignments.

Mutual Respect

Student groups are more likely to work effectively if they have mutual respect. Mutual respect will also reduce negative and discriminatory feelings. Effective groups are also noticeable by balanced participation. When impartial participation occurs, all students in a group are contributing to the discussion or project in which they are involved.

As they listen to each other, they display a frequent uptake of ideas when responding to peer ideas and accepting and building on them through further discussion, This can also be achieved by engaging students in constructive argumentation when they are not in agreement. Finally, students in collaborative learning groups should also engage in high-quality strategies that are both social and cognitive.

Problem Solving

Collaborative problem solving usually requires more planning and consumes more time than individual problem solving. Instructors cannot take for granted that their students will have a readily accessible protocol for solving problems and must often outline a process or provide a checklist of achievement steps. The method by which groups are selected and roles assigned within those groups will need to be considered. The task or problem to be studied and the criteria for measuring task accomplishment need to be clearly explained to the students. See appendix D for more information on problem solving.

Group Cognitive Strategy

A great deal of research has focused on the cognitive strategy to be used in group activity. This research concluded that students who employ high level cognitive strategies such as elaboration, explanation, and coordinating theories in group assignments learn more from collaborative work than students who do not employ these strategies. Noreen Webb (2012) and her colleagues produced a very noteworthy body of work that emphasized the significance of providing and receiving explanations during group activities.

Their research provided this example: if students are working on mathematics problems in groups, when a student explains to another student how to solve a problem, or how to carry out some of the steps in problem solving, the giver of the explanation typically benefits more than the receiver. The receiver of the explanation may benefit if the explanation is sufficiently elaborated on and if the receiver applies what was learned to other situations. In contrast, "terminal help" occurs when a student simply tells another student the answer. Thus, terminal help can often be harmful to learning.

Webb's research has pointed to the importance of designing collaborative learning formats in ways that increase the frequency of explanations in group work and decrease the frequency of terminal help. Chinn (2006) offered another type of highly productive strategy that provided an alternative point of view on these issues: advanced reasoning and evidence, Chin concluded that students benefit from encountering ideas that are different from their own, and they gain a deeper understanding of ideas that they are learning when they consider how these ideas are related to evidence for and against those ideas.

Group Evaluation

Robert Slavin (1990–1996) is the most well-known proponent of the use of reward structures to encourage learning in groups. Slavin's research has differentiated three methods for assigning rewards to a group. The first is that the entire group can receive a reward for its performance (e.g., all group members are given the same grade on each group project). However, this approach does not endorse positive interdependence in that the most skilled students often do most of the work to ensure high grades, while some students fail to apply equal effort in task achievement.

In the second method he proposed students work together in a group, but are given individual grades. This method discourages social loafing because each group member is individually evaluated, but it provides no reason for students to work as a group. Also, he pointed out that students can receive group rewards based on individual improvement on quizzes or worksheets. For example, students might receive a group reward based on the average individual improvement on an English quiz to be taken as a result of the participation in collaborative work. This provides incentives for students to help each other.

The most proficient students will want to help the less proficient students because their reward depends partly on the performance of those students on the quiz. The less proficient students have an incentive to collaborate in order not to let the group down. Third, Slavin has recommended that rewards for average group improvement not be grades. The use of rewards in group work is controversial because many researchers have argued that tangible rewards undermine intrinsic motivation (Johnson and Johnson, 1991).

Barbara Millis, a faculty director at the Air Force Academy concluded that peer evaluation builds team skills in that it allows students to reflect on their involvement in the process, progress, and outcomes in addition to providing the instructor with continuous feedback. She further recommends that, after a group assignment, evaluations be followed up by students answering the following questions:

- Did all members of the group contribute?
- What could be done in the next group assignment to make the group better?
- What important factors and things did the student learn?
- What contributions did each student make that made the group more efficient?

Millis indicates there are three levels of evaluation that can and should be used in evaluating group performance: First, peer (individual) evaluations can be used several times during the group process. Second are would-be group evaluations in which the group evaluates one another's contribution and performance. This is achieved by students writing individual reports and comments regarding each individual's contribution to group performance. They should criticize individual peers' work in addition to providing positive feedback with suggestions for improvement in certain areas. The last form of evaluation consists of the instructor's evaluation of both group and individual achievement.

This evaluation could be accomplished by instructor observations, written essays, and subject matter exams. Individual evaluation can consist of a subject matter test/exam or essay. Group evaluation would include the performance of the entire group. Below are essential goals to be achieved as a result of COLL participation. These goals result from various studies by researchers and educators that indicated that a conceptual understanding of the content being studied should be achieved by each individual in a group. The ability to use comprehension, reasoning, problem solving, critical thinking, and cognitive approaches will aid each member of the group to become more proficient:

1. Social behavior and the ability of each individual member to work proficiently within the group setting should be established.
2. The ability to value and respect their peers, create friendship, and appreciate diversity are goals that all student members must cultivate.
3. These processes occur when groups are engaged in the task at hand and interested in the task achievement. If this occurs, students are naturally less likely to fall into off-task behavior or social loafing.
4. Student engagement is increased when they are given more control of the process of group achievement, rather than individual outcomes. This can be accomplished by allowing students to have a choice in learning activities and decision-making situations.

Interdependence

Johnson and Johnson (1990) have emphasized the importance of positive interdependence, which occurs when students complete a task by working together on a task that cannot be completed as effectively or at all when working individually. Effective positive interdependence is then likely to result in joint attention to the tasks at hand (Barron, 2003). Interdependence means that students are focused on the same task, looking at the same information, and generally talking about common topics.

A designated goal for any group activity should be to build strong positive group interdependence, which means a "one for all and all for one" camaraderie that encourages members to help each other work toward common goals. This can be as simple as offering bonus points to a study group if everyone in the group scores above a certain minimum grade on assignments, tests, or individual papers. The results will motivate the better prepared students to help and encourage the members who are most likely not going to meet their goals, and the less prepared students are likely to work harder so as not to disappoint the group.

Chinn (2006) concluded that students benefit from encountering ideas that are different from their own, and they gain a deeper understanding of the ideas they are learning when they consider how statements are related to evidence for and against those assertions. Additional instructional formats (learning skills, group development, problems solving, independent thinking, and critical thinking for collaborative learning) can be found in appendix D.

KEY IDEAS TO REMEMBER

Collaborative learning is said to encompass all approaches to learning, and the research viewed concluded that COLL is based on the idea that there exists an inherent social nature of learning found in all students. Research further concluded the following key concepts to remember:

- Student learning is based on the idea that learning takes place best in natural social events where the participants talk among themselves.
- It is through deliberation that learning takes place.
- Collaborative learning develops a quicker assessment of a certain amount of resource material.
- It creates the capacity to apply and share knowledge and principles that increase student understanding of complex concepts while improving the ability to solve problems.
- This learning process leads to enhanced creativity and understanding of different perspectives and improved management of prejudice and bias.
- It leads to increased diversity and valuing that develops positive attitudes toward learning.
- Fosters meta-cognition in that student are involved in recognition and analysis of how to learn.

Chapter Six

Constructivist Learning Theory

Collaborative learning (COLL) refers to any instructional method that places students in groups who work toward common goals and that emphasizes student interaction to solve problems. Neuroscience supports constructivism (CONS) as a natural way people actively learn. Thus, experimental learning is attained through interactive learning that engages and expands the educational experience. The procedures required to educate students must provide the following:

- real life experiences;
- exploration;
- thinking;
- reflection;
- interaction with the environment; and
- experiences that construct and cultivate knowledge.

Constructivism, according to scientific investigation, establishes an educational process that is not based on what the teacher has to offer but is a natural process spontaneously carried out by students. Therefore, learning is not acquired by listening to dialogue from an instructor, but by experiences present in the environment. Thus, the learner must become self-directed, creative, and innovative. Therefore, the purpose of this educational system is for students to become imaginative and original through analysis, conceptualization, and synthesis of previous information in order to create new knowledge.

Therefore, educators have come to realize that students should construct their own knowledge. Thus, the constructivist theory of learning was developed and states that learning is an active process that will create knowledge from environmental experiences. This presumption concludes that students learn best by making sense of information on their own as the instructor becomes a facilitator in the learning process. Constructivism is a learning process that allows students to experience environmental situations firsthand, thereby giving the student experiences in learning that provides them with reliable knowledge.

Once learning is achieved, the student is required to act upon the knowledge obtained and test its reliability. In constructivism, the learner is responsible for their own motivation and learning while the instructor becomes a facilitator of learning rather than a dispenser of information/knowledge. In this method, student learning becomes an active and social process while the dynamics of interaction between instructor and learner changes as students collaborate in determining the content to be learned. In this process the scope and sequence of subject matter should be discovered by engaging and challenging the learner.

Neuroscience now supports active learning as the way people naturally learn. Active learning that is constructive has been found to be a most effective method for creating knowledge through experimental learning. Education through active learning will engage and expand a student's educational experiences by providing for exploration, thinking, and reflection through interaction with educators and other students in a learning environment.

This process allows students to experience real-life situations. Science has established that learning is not what the teacher gives, but a natural spontaneous process that takes place in individuals who listen to words spoken by an instructor and use them when they experience situations in the environment.

A student involved in active/constructive learning becomes self-directed, creative, and innovative through analysis, conception, and synthesis, which create knowledge. Hein's (2013) research, in trying to establish "what is constructivism," determined that there was nothing dramatically new that differs from what was put forward by Dewey. However, there is a new widespread acceptance of these old set ideas, and there is cognitive psychological research to justify it. In determining what constructivism is, Dewey came to the following conclusion: the term refers to the idea that learners construct knowledge for themselves in that each learner individually and socially constructs knowledge as he or she learns.

Students cooperate in a positive way by sharing responsibility for assigned activities and goal achievement. Furthermore, every student in a group is expected to contribute equally. Hein's research also found that the motivation to learn depends heavily on the learner's confidence in his or her potential for learning, which is improved by learning to solve problems and by experiencing successful conclusions of challenging tasks. He found that as a result of these experiences students are more motivated to take part in future complex challenges. A few strategies for constructive learning include students working together to ask and answer questions and solve problems.

Therefore, each student involved in team assignments becomes an expert and teaches others in their group who are having difficulty. In addition, each student works in a team situation to research and make rational decisions. In active CONS learning, students perform as a group in order to reach agreement and understanding while discovering principles, concepts, and facts for themselves that could not otherwise be achievable. Student knowledge is a product of a student's social nature, culture, and the group process that occurs through social reaction to events in the environment.

A dynamic interactive process occurs between instructor and learners that requires the students and the instructor to develop an awareness of each other's point of view, which will improve their association. Collaboration and elaboration results when learners work together to develop an understanding of information and knowledge that would be nearly impossible to obtain singlehandedly. Active learners discover principles, concepts, and facts and share their perceptive thinking with teammates.

HOW STUDENTS LEARN IN A CONSTRUCTIVE ENVIRONMENT

In order to understand the constructivist and other theories of teaching included in this book requires the instructor to know and understand how students learn best. Constructivists believe that student learning is most successful if the instructors understand that learning is an interactive process for constructing or creating importance from a variety of experiences. Better still, instruction must be based on the student trying to create and perceive results regarding his or her own efforts, with the instructor acting as a facilitator who guides them through the instructional process.

Various instructional strategies indicate that interactive constructive learning is best accomplished with a hands-on approach based on experimentation with students making their own inferences, discoveries, and conclusions. Furthermore, instructors and learners are equally involved in learning from each other, which indicates that the learning experience is both subjective and objective.

This process requires the instructor's values and background to be an essential part of interplay between students, the instructor, and the task to be achieved. To make it simple, learning is a two-way process between learners and between learners and the facilitator who provides the basic ideas that should be formulated prior to and through the entire learning process.

The facilitator should structure the procedures to be used based on his or her knowledge (sensory input) that is structured by the student receiving the stimulus. Therefore, information must be processed by the student's brain, making it difficult to transfer information directly from the facilitator to the learner and be processed correctly. The facilitator's assessment of active learning requires that they view learning as a continuous and interactive process with a complex myriad of facts, problems, dimensions, and perceptions when measuring achievement. Consequently, students learn more effectively and efficiently if they construct knowledge for themselves.

NDT Resources Center researched and assembled a list of teaching methods that produce the highest retention rates. Below is a list that shows which methods have the greatest retention rate and which would also be a factor in the other learning methods included in this research.

1. Immediate use of learning to teaching others—90 percent
2. Practice by doing—75 percent
3. Discussion groups—50 percent
4. Demonstration—30 percent
5. Audiovisual—20 percent
6. Reading—10 percent
7. Lecture—5 percent

THE NATURE OF THE LEARNER

The objective of constructive learning is to develop self-directed, creative, and innovative analysis of how students learn to conceptualize and synthesis prior experiences in order to create new knowledge. Glasersfeld (1989) concluded the responsibility of learning remains exclusively with the learner, while the student remains actively involved in the learning process. This researcher concluded that the learner's motivation to learn is strongly dependent on his or her confidence and potential for learning.

Therefore, the ability to solve problems is based on the confidence that is derived from a student's past problem-solving ability. Those who are pushed to improve their ability slightly above their current level of knowledge tend to be more motivated to perform. The learning environment should be designed to challenge the learner's thinking and knowledge

THE BENEFITS OF CONSTRUCTIVISM

In deciding which method of teaching will provide the most effective and efficient education, educators must look at the beneficial versus negative factors with the most important factor being the student's ability to retain material learned. According to research in student retention, science has established that education is a natural process by which students learn, not by listening to words, but by experiences received through interaction. Montessori advocated learning as a process which gives students experience in an environment and provides students with reliable knowledge.

Kolb's (1994) studies emphasized that conditional knowledge is gained through experimental learning and pointed out that concrete experiences are a part of the learning progression in which students encounter experiences. This makes it possible for them to act within the environment to test their knowledge and gives them reliable and trustworthy answers. Vygotsky showed that reality is a descriptive construction in the student's imagination. He stressed the importance of establishing mechanisms for mutual planning, diagnosis of learner needs, and building interest in a cooperative learning climate, as well as activities that achieve their objectives.

CRITICISM OF EDUCATIONAL CONSTRUCTIVISM

Constructivist learning has been criticized by some educators who question the "learning by doing and discovery" method of instruction because there appears to be little empirical evidence that supports this instructional theory. These educators believe that novice learners have to develop their own mental ability. Mayer (2004) indicates that discovery-teaching tactics used by constructivists are inefficient or effective due to the learner's active behavior and that guided discovery should be used instead. He further states that learners should be cognitively active during learning and that guided practice should always be used.

In contrast, Kitschier (2006) indicated that "constructivist methods were unguided" methods of instruction in that they were too structured and that problem solving and inquiry would be ineffective because students are provided no guidance and support. Slezak found that constructivism is a doctrine that can have little benefit for practical pedagogy or teaching. This researcher also stated that constructivist teaching methods were unguided methods of instruction due to the learner's inexperience.

Myer's (2004) research argues that not all constructive techniques are suitable and effective for all learners in that educators misapply constructivism by making it an active behavior. There appears to be confusion about how constructivist learning theory is viewed, and it is often compared to social constructivism, which is associated with a higher order of learning that requires mature learners.

INSTRUCTORS AS A FACILITATOR

In a constructivist approach to teaching, the role of instructor changes to that of a facilitator of instruction and knowledge. As a facilitator of knowledge, the objective is to aid learners in achieving their own understanding of course content. The facilitator plays a passive role, with students assuming an active function in the learning process. The instructor as a facilitator develops a different set of skills, while in the past the teacher acted as a dispenser of information. Meanwhile, the facilitator acts as a consultant who provides guidelines and creates an environment that allows the learner to arrive at their own conclusions.

A facilitator designs a supportive and challenging environment that requires students to think critically in solving problems. A facilitator also establishes a learning environment that is designed to give learners ownership of the process of problem solving to reach the correct decisions. Social constructivists believe that each student shares the point of view that collaborative elaboration will result in the learners building content understanding that could not be achieved individually. As a form of interactive learning, CONS learning should include the following factors:

- reciprocal teaching;
- peer collaborate;
- cognitive apprenticeship;
- problem solving instruction;
- anchored instruction.

Constructivists believe that learners with different skills and experiences should collaborate in solving tasks through discussions that arrive at shared understandings. Constructivists also believe that the instructor and learner should see assessment as a continuous process that continually measures the achievement of student performance. Feedback created by the assessment process should be used to provide for further development and learning. Learners should be challenged with tasks that require skills slightly beyond the students' current level of ability, which creates the motivation needed to increase the efforts that were built on previous success.

The educator's role is as a mentor who aids students in solving problems that may modify existing knowledge to create new knowledge. Wertsch (1970) states that social constructivism recognizes the uniqueness and complexity of the learner and supports the instructor's role in active learning, as a mentor for learning and problem solving that modifies existing knowledge and that leads to the creation of new learning. This process enables students to learn throughout their lives and enhances the nature of the learner's social interaction with knowledgeable members of society.

An example of the interactive process can be seen in young children who learn through interaction with other children, adults, and the outside world. The instructor's function is to observe and direct discussion, which is an essential part of the learning process, while making sense of it according to his or her current conceptions. Therefore, students learn best when they are allowed to construct a personal understanding based on experiencing things and reflecting on those experiences

Characteristics of Constructivist Teaching

One of the primary goals of using constructivist teaching is for students to learn by training them in taking the initiative for their own learning experiences. The characteristics of a constructivist classroom are:

- The learners are actively involved.
- The environment is democratic.
- The activities are interactive and student-centered.
- Teachers facilitate a process of learning in which students are encouraged to be responsible and autonomous.

Suggestions for improving constructive instruction are as follows:

- Encourage and accept student autonomy and initiative.
- Try to use raw data and primary sources, in addition to manipulative, interactive, and physical materials.
- When assigning tasks for students, facilitators use cognitive terminology such as "classify," "analyze," "predict," and "create."
- Build off and use student responses when making "on-the-spot" decisions about teacher behaviors, instructional strategies, activities, and content to be taught.
- Search out students' understanding of prior experiences about a concept before teaching it to them.
- Encourage communication between the teacher and the students and also among the students.
- Promote student critical thinking and inquiry ability by asking them thoughtful, open-ended questions, and persuade them to ask questions of each other.
- Ask follow-up questions and seek elaboration after a student's initial response.
- Put students in situations that might challenge their previous conceptions that create contradictions that will encourage discussion.
- Make sure to wait long enough after posing a question so that the students have time to think about their answers and be able to respond thoughtfully.
- Provide enough time for students to construct their own meaning when learning something new.

Additional group development, problem solving, independent- and critical-thinking data can be found in appendix D.

KEY IDEAS TO REMEMBER

Neuroscience supports constructivism CONS as a natural way people actively learn. Thus, experimental learning is attained through interactive learning that engages and expands the educational experience. Constructivism, according to scientific investigation, establishes an educational process that is not based on what the teacher has to offer, but is a natural process spontaneously carried out by students. Therefore, educators must come to realize that students should construct their own knowledge. The constructivist theory of learning was developed and states that learning is an active process that will create knowledge from environmental experiences. This process includes:

- A student involved in active/constructive learning becomes self-directed, creative, and innovative through analysis, conception, and synthesis that create knowledge.
- Student knowledge is a product of a student's social nature, culture, and the group process that occurs through social reaction to events in the environment.
- A dynamic interactive process occurs between instructor and learners that requires students and the instructor to develop an awareness of each other's point of view in order to improve their association.
- Constructivists believe that student learning is most successful if the instructors understand that learning is an interactive process for constructing or creating importance from a variety of experiences.
- The facilitator should structure the procedures to be used based on the knowledge (sensory input) that is structured by the student receiving the stimulus.
- One of the primary goals of using constructivist teaching methods is for students to learn how to learn by training them in taking the initiative for their own learning experiences.

Chapter Seven

Student Centered Learning

THE BASIC CONCEPTS

As educational practices evolve, so does the approach to teaching and learning. The great thing about education is that the mindset about teaching and learning is constantly evolving with new and novel ways to teach and reach diverse learners. A student-centered learning (SCL) approach to teaching focuses on the needs of students by making them responsible for learning and by reducing their reliance on other students, to teachers, and administrators. Student-centered learning allows the students to be autonomous in their learning by reducing the reliance on the teacher (Wright University).

Through this process, student learning now becomes based on personal learning goals by creating, in conjunction with class requirements, a change in how the curriculum produces knowledge. Simply put, students are allowed to learn on their own with minimal teacher intervention and supervision. The results are that students spend the majority of class time constructing a new understanding of the materials being studied, which is a proactive approach.

This progression places the student at the center of the learning process, as the major factor in acquiring knowledge, while the instructor becomes a facilitator of learning. This situation also puts the student interests and abilities at the forefront of a learning course of action that establishes students as the major factor in acquiring knowledge and making lessons meaningful. Students, based on their own learning goals that are determined in conjunction with class requirements, produce a need to change the curriculum in order to construct new knowledge.

The instructor at this point becomes a working partner, an intellectual contributor, and a resource of knowledge in a course of action that puts students' interests and abilities at the forefront in learning advancement.

Let's not forget that the key to motivating students to learn and explore innovative learning methods is to create an environment that is fun and interesting. Once the student's attention has been captured, lessons become personalized by opportunity to use their own learning style and innate abilities to attain and comprehend acquired concepts.

The function of the subject matter presented in SCL is to cultivate a vigorous knowledge base while developing learning proficiency and improving learner awareness. The instructor then becomes another resource for information as students develop the skills to become active and responsible for what they learn. In SCL, students work in partnership with the instructor and other students to construct knowledge, which is the indirect opposite of instructor-centered learning (traditional approach) that ignores and suppresses the learner's responsibilities (Armstrong 2012). This new method of learning can now focus on how students learn, while making use of each student's style of learning.

Based on the theories of John Dewey, Jean Piaget, and Lev Vygotsky, focus is now directed to how students learn and indicate that students must become active participants in the discovery of information and learning procedures. Class time is now spent developing knowledge and understanding the material being learned in a proactive course of action. Student-centered learning provides a better lifelong learning environment, in that it provides students with the tools and methodologies that give rise to higher student motivation, in and out of the classroom, allowing learning to become the incentive for performance success.

Since what is learned is self-discovered; students begin to utilize self-regulated procedures. Carl Rogers proposed a theory that "the only learning which significantly influences behavior and education is self-discovered." The instructor, by initiating these new teaching strategies, enables students to make inquires that set the stage for their academic success while creating improved and productive activities and abilities. This openness of the learning atmosphere establishes a cooperative/collaborative learning environment that provides students with the prospect of exploring their own learning style.

Active learning constructs learning by engaging students fully in a learning course of action. The instructor's responsibility becomes that of a facilitator of learning, as opposed to a dispenser of information that enables students to experience content: as Carl Rogers (1969) stated, "significant learning is acquired through being active and doing things."

Although the requirements of the curriculum remain the same, students study and learn to create and apply their newfound knowledge. Therefore, learning is enhanced when students cooperate in deciding how to display this new body of knowledge they have acquired through their learning objectives. The learner now becomes responsible for acquiring knowledge, leaving the facilitator to evaluate the learner with timely individual feedback and self-discovery. According to James Henderson (1992), there are three objectives of SCL: subject learning, self-learning, and social learning created through peer-to-peer interaction and collaborative thinking that improve curriculum knowledge.

Likewise, Vygotsky (1987) indicated that students learn vicariously through interaction with each other. In SCL, lecturing to students is not completely ignored in that the fascinator is an expert in the subject being taught. With this in mind, instructors must be allowed some time for explaining, clarifying, demonstrating, and discussing relevant information together with students. Furthermore, lecture-centered learning can increase a student's ability to obtain more information by the end of the quarter/semester, while the facilitator and students will also see evidence that a greater level of learning has taken place.

The following are a few examples put forth by Wikipedia.com, that display the reasoning that points out the rationale of why SCL should be intergraded into today's curriculum:

- Students are more motivated to learn.
- Peer communication is highly promoted.
- Students' disruptive and unacceptable behavior is reduced.
- Better student-teacher relationship are constructed.
- Discovery and active learning are encouraged.
- Students assume responsibility for their own learning.

Student-centered learning consists of actively learning course-related material in which all students are called upon to be actively engaged during class activities. The focus of SCL is on needs, abilities, interests, and learning styles and acknowledges the students as the main factor in the learning experience. This learning methodology centers on the students' ability to choose how they will learn, what they will learn, and how they will be facilitator-assessed as well as assessing their own learning.

Therefore, active learning in a teacher-centered class only takes place when the instructor asks questions, poses a problem, or issues information for discussion that challenges student learning. Armstrong (2012) stated that "traditional education ignores and suppresses learner responsibility."

Students in SCL work in small groups as a system for coming up with responses to the questions asked or problems proposed. Once this is accomplished, students are asked to share their responses, first within their groups and then with the class as a whole. Active learning does not occur when the instructor lectures to the class followed by only a few students answering proposed questions that are discussed by a small fraction of the class. The instructor in active learning does not eliminate lecturing altogether but spends less time in the lecturing process.

Instructors can limit lecture time to simply telling students what they should know and explain information to be learned while clarifying demonstrations and models relevant to the activity being studied. Class activities in SCL are limited only by the students' and instructors' imaginations. An interactive student-centered learning process begins by asking students questions, explaining complex concepts, developing flow charts/diagrams/timelines, and by brainstorming to solve problems by setting realistic performance goals. In SCL, the instructor should only direct class activities that focus on problems for students to solve that take place in the real world.

Research indicates that students learn much more by doing things and getting feedback as soon as possible. When classes are lively and enjoyable, interest in the learning process increases and the quality of information that can be dealt with improves dramatically. In addition, fitting the difficulty of a task to the skill and ability of the student makes for more positive learning. The National Research Council (1999) recommended organizing learning environments into the four following learning strategies:

- Knowledge-centered learning: This stresses the development of student knowledge in order to facilitate transfer of information learned to a new context and uses this application of that knowledge to the challenges presented by problem solving and critical thinking activities.
- Learner-centered: McCombs and Whistler (1997) stated that learners must be treated as co-creators in the ideas and issues that deserve attention and consideration.
- Assessment-centered: This learning environment recognizes the importance of prior knowledge and its influence on future learning. This process provides opportunities for feedback which leads to evaluation and judgment of the learning process
- Community-centered: This learning environments recognizes that individual learners take many cues and insights from other learners that promote and sustain their learning process. This learning procedure facilitates purposeful interaction among students and success is determined by both student and instructor assessments.

TEACHER'S ROLE AS A FACILITATOR

As previously stated, in the SCL process, students are positioned at the center of learning, and that becomes a major factor in acquiring knowledge, while the instructor becomes a facilitator of learning. This process puts the student's interests and abilities first, while the instructor becomes responsible for creating a learning atmosphere that motivates students to accept SCL. Ideally, the teacher's role inside the classroom is to facilitate learning (as an organizer, guide, and synthesizer of knowledge) by allowing the students to have a say and use their abilities and learning style to absorb and make meaning out of the lessons to be learned.

The major question teachers must ask themselves is, how can I move from teacher-centered to student-centered learning? First, teachers must understand that by using the SCL approach to teaching never means that teachers do not lecture or have no control of the class. It just means they have less traditional teaching responsibilities. Teachers, by instituting a slow attentive and reflective transition to SCL, will most likely end up with sustainable changes in their teaching methods.

The following are directions teachers might take: 1) begin by using a small number of teaching methods; 2) consider using a few informal cooperative learning structures, 3) engage students in their assignments after lecturing for a short portion of the class as suggested by Cooper and Robinson (2000).

Faculty members might begin with informal cooperative learning approaches such as: think-pair-share (Lynam 1981), Quick-thinks (Johnston and Cooper (1997), and one-minute papers (Angelo and Cross (1993), to name a few. Krima Olive Molina in her "Best Practices for SCL" suggests a constructivist approach that involves and allows students to experience learning by initiating the following key procedures:

- Place students' interests, intellectually and emotionally, at the forefront.
- Allow students to use their unique learning styles to maximize learning, with the teacher using the scaffolding procedure at the proper time.
- Use students' interests as the basis for motivation.
- Enable students to use their personalized learning styles.
- Place students into diverse groups/teams that advocate discovery through active learning.
- Place emphasis on responsibility and accountability.
- Insure the use of positive constructive feedback.
- Support self-awareness and reflection in group work.
- Advance student's social, peer, communication, and collaborative attitudes.

To reduce problems that might occur, the instructor can move from a teacher-centered to student-centered classroom in stages. Lynam, (1981), developed a SCL process by beginning with a simple student-centered learning approach to teaching. This process got underway by asking students to think individually about a question for a few minutes, then turn to a neighbor and exchange ideas. Once this was completed, he randomly selected a small number of students to share their ideas with their class/team that consisted of three-to-five-student groups taking part in individual discussions, followed by a discussion within the entire class.

Next, a roundtable approach could be instituted by asking questions to student groups/teams. The first student writes and shares her or his answer by passing it to a second student, and so on until it reaches each student in the group. Additional discussion can take place by students discussing and sharing their ideas with the class. Leaner-centered education places the student at the center of education, which begins with understanding the educational contexts from which a student comes. It continues with the instructor evaluating the student's progress toward their learning objectives.

By being helped to acquire the basic skills of learning, the student is ultimately provided with a basis for learning throughout life. This process places the responsibility for learning squarely on the student's shoulders, while the instructor assumes responsibility for overseeing the student's education. This approach strives to be individualistic, flexible, competency based, and varied in methodology that is not always constrained by time or place. Many student-centered approaches to learning employ the instructors to form small student groups/teams of four to five students to conduct and construct learning activities.

In addition to knowing how to develop a healthy classroom environment, teachers will need to understand how students function effectively and become productive in a group/team environment. This is accomplished by students completing assigned tasks that require the development of individual accountability and responsibility.

ASSESSMENT

One of the most fundamental distinctions between student-centered and teacher-centered learning is assessment. Researchers in student-centered learning have concluded that assessment is not solely an exam students take at the end of a unit. They believe that it is a part of all three learning components: which include the content, product, and process. Since assessment is an ongoing performance-based process, students need multiple opportunities to demonstrate what knowledge they have learned.

Evaluation has been defined as the process by which data is collected through assessment. Effective evaluation requires the teacher to gather information regarding achievement in order to know what to re-teach and when students need greater challenges. In student-centered learning, the learners contribute to a knowledge process that engages students in assessment to determine their own progress and in deciding what factors should be assessed. This is followed by how to exhibit what they have learned. Developing a student-assessment process that sustains learning will increase motivation.

However, the acceptance of a new system of learning by parents, teachers, and administrators has been difficult to achieve when compared to the level of thinking and the skills taught in the traditional classroom. In addition, a question that is often asked by parents and administrators is: Does SCL assessment accurately measure learning? Since the evaluation process in SCL is different from traditional learning, judgments have to be made regarding the following factors:

- Have students achieved the learning goals set for themselves?
- What are the relative strengths and weaknesses of the assessment process?
- Are there changes that need to be made in developing goals and learning strategies?

In traditional leaning, grades are generally based on what students have learned as measured by tests, papers, projects, presentation, and goal achievement. Therefore, grades will be impacted by student efforts, attitude, behavior, and participation, in addition to class requirements of attendance and turning work in on time. However, it should be recognized that the greatest motivation for learning is learning itself. If a student can make the transition from extrinsic rewards (recognition, grades, etc.) to intrinsic rewards, then the basis for lifelong learning will have been established.

There is a certain joy in learning that is associated with knowing and predicting how the world works. According to Parkinson (1999), students in SCL classes have opportunities to experience intrinsic types of learning situations. If student learning is determined by their grades on achievement tests, quizzes, and papers, they come too late for teachers to make adjustments in instruction to improve student understanding, content mastery, and skill development.

However, adopting alternate approaches to student evaluation will improve teaching and student learning. Columbia University adopted the following four principles that can be used for assessing SCL learning:

1. The objectives of learning to be achieved should be based on assessment. This includes what the students need to know, what the class is trying to accomplish, and the content and skills to be achieved.
2. Assessment requires instruction to be specific about the outcomes being assessed.
3. The objectives of instruction must be student focused.
4. The outcomes of learning must be measurable.

Assessment should take place throughout the learning process, instead of at the end of the process, in order to determine what is being learned and what is needed to improve learning and who needs help. Columbia University also suggested the following four factors that will enable instructors to adjust their teaching and assessment procedures.

1. Develop small groups so that the students can be observed and changes made when needed.
2. Give students problems to solve and have them articulate what they are doing.
3. Efficient diagnosis of student strength and weakness can often be achieved by having them write one-minute-paper assignments to demonstrate competency.
4. Enable each student to assess their own competency by allowing them to evaluate what they have learned, and compare it with the instructor's observations and curriculum responsibilities.

In order for students to demonstrate what they have learned, assessment must be effective in determining if students achievement has taken place and how to improve weakness in the curriculum and provide for feedback. In addition, assessment should challenge students to take ownership of their learning and determine if what they are learning relates to course objectives and if they are meeting these class objectives

Assessment for feedback and improvement is referred to as a *formative* assessment, which can promote the development of capacities and attitudes that can last students for a lifetime. Meanwhile, assessment for conclusive evaluation and judgment is referred to as *summative* assessment. However, if the main purpose of assessment is summative as a means of grading performance, promoting learning and improving student's participation as the process should be one in which students evaluate their own learning.

The objective is to determine what the students really know and have learned in relation to class assignments. With this in mind, a variety of assessment procedures need to be made available to instructors and students in order to appeal to each student's learning styles.

BENEFITS

There are tremendous advantages to teachers and students involved in SCL in that students will cultivate learning and develop new skills while gaining the importance of knowing that acquiring knowledge is a lifelong process. Student-centered learning promotes an integrated curriculum that reinforces student motivation, promotes peer communication, and reduces disruptive behavior. In addition, this method of learning builds better student-instructor relationships, promotes discovery by active learning, and shifts the responsibility for learning away from the instructor to the students.

Teachers benefit from a reduction in the amount of the traditional learning workload they faced in the past. Teachers in SCL reported significant increases in the use of methods that involved students actively in their learning. Group work, practical work, projects and assignments, and simulations and role playing are used more in SCL than in the past. Many teachers now allow students to advance at their own pace. In addition, recent research has found that over 60 percent of teachers are now using "whole class" teaching, with traditional learning playing a smaller role. Both students and teaching staffs reported frequent use of diagnostic assessment as an aid in teaching and learning.

On the whole, teachers and students welcome the changes in learning that have taken place. While students appreciated the new emphasis on practical work, projects, assignments, and diagnostic assessment they express thoughts that anything is better than chalk-talk because they feel what happens in SCL is learned better and more deeply than in previous learning methods. Studies by Collins and O'Brien (2003) found that properly executed SCL can lead to increased motivation to learn, greater retention of knowledge, deeper understandings, and a positive attitude toward the subject being taught.

Below is a review of what research indicates as advantages for both teacher and students. Student-centered learning plays a major role in the educational process if the following key ideas are remembered:

- It strengthens learning and other skills in addition to knowledge that will improve student learning throughout their lifetime.
- It creates the possibility for students to learn their relationships and responsibilities.
- Students discover that learning is fun and worthwhile.
- Students become more attentive and willing to participate openly in learning situations.
- Criticism regarding irrelevance and unfairness is greatly reduced.
- Constructs/increases teacher knowledge about students work and learning that creates improvement in teacher evaluations.
- Teaching and student learning become more interesting and fun.
- It develops a basic active-learning structure that make teachers planning activities more effective and efficient.
- It creates profound thinking skills and attitudes that are important to critical thinking and problem solving.
- It increases student participation in class activities that are achieved by taking part in discussions as groups and as individual students.

- It reinforces student motivation and expands peer communication.
- It decreases disruptive behavior.
- It generates better student-teacher relationships.
- It supports discovery and active learning.
- Students develop responsibility for their own learning.
- it improves problem solving and critical thinking.

DISADVANTAGES

While many teachers welcomed student-centered learning wholeheartedly, others classified factors that preclude its full use. Chief among these were time, resources, and independent learning. Traditionalists state that instruction is more efficient when it consists of a single, unified curriculum for all students regardless of their ability or interest. In addition, traditionalists, such as Herried (1998), claim that SCL is hindered in that the learners must be trained in the goals, objectives, methodologies, and implementation of assessment techniques.

Research has found that the following are reasons listed by teachers who have not completely accepted SCL with statements such as:

- Student-centered learning is an ineffective approach to learning due to limit on time allowed.
- Chalk-and-talk continue to be used in that it is a relatively efficient and a quick method of communicating information.
- Teachers are hesitant to commit themselves entirely to SCL in that they felt that some students are not ready to take on the added responsibility.
- Some students experience difficulty due to lack of ability to work on their own.
- There is some substantiation that few students were fully aware of their learning styles.
- Lower-ability-level students have problems relating to this new approach to learning in that they have little knowledge of the teamwork process which is too complicated.
- Teachers fail to understand that they are preparing students for the real world,
- Assessment may not reveal what a student has learned.
- Grading standards are often not in agreement.

Faculty members often have many questions about the SCL approach and its implications regarding how they might teach. The following are several of these questions:

- Are teachers able to cover course content in their syllabus?
- Can student-centered learning be used when teaching large classes?
- Is it possible to move from teacher-centered to student-centered in stages?
- Will teachers be able to respond to poor student behavior?

GROUP/TEAMWORK

SCL is based on a group/team effort, and students must understand the conditions within their group and the process they must undertake in order to accomplish their assigned tasks, both in groups and in the classroom. Critical to a healthy group environment is an effective process based on strong communication skills. Below you will find the basic characteristics of effective communicators, plus tips to help student groups establish a healthy atmosphere and learning process. Although students can gain many of the skills illustrated below through informal social interactions, they will best benefit from making a clear-cut effort to perfect their communication skills.

Students will also need opportunities to practice giving as well as receiving regular feedback on how they're doing by sharing information within their groups and classroom. Students set activities for their group/team, while working in incorporation to achieve the three elements of feedback. Reflective group discussions and/or peer assessment also includes self-reflection. In order to function successfully in a small group, students need to be able to communicate intellectually with emotion and clarity.

Research indicates that effective communication can be established if:

- The students clarify their own ideas during communication.
- They communicate their opinions in an open but nonthreatening manner.
- They listen carefully to other students and the instructor.
- They ask questions to clarify other students' ideas and emotions.
- They sense how others feel about their lack of ability to communicate verbally.
- They initiate conversations about a groups' environment or process if tensions occur.
- They reflect on the activities and interactions within their group/team by encouraging other group members to improve their ability to communicate.

Regular open communication, in which group members share their thoughts, ideas, and feelings, is a must for successful group/team work. Unspoken assumptions and issues can be very damaging when someone is attempting to develop productive group functioning. When students are willing to communicate openly with one another, a healthy climate takes place, and an effective learning process will transpire. Skills for a healthy environment require students to work together successfully as group members and demonstrate a sense of unity.

Cohesion takes place as group members exhibit the qualities of 1) openness in which group members are willing to get to know each another, generally those with dissimilar interests and backgrounds, 2) openness to new ideas, varied viewpoints, and the diversity of individuals in attendance, 3) willingness to listen to others and agree with their ideas, 4) knowledge in advance of how to balance the need for cohesion within the group as well as the need for individual articulation, 5) trust and self-disclosure, in which group members are willing to share ideas, and 6) each member encouraging self-awareness and being reflective of the significance of group work.

One of the most important things an instructor can do in developing group and class teamwork is to have students regularly contemplate their group experiences. This self-expression will reinforce and further develop critical teamwork skills that are based on the goals and the objectives of group projects that allow students to construct questions to be talked about within the team. Students can then add these questions to their journal about their responses to the group environment and process as it takes place.

Journals that support self-reflection can help students see teamwork issues as a new way to initiate ideas for group resolution. They can also provide a good basis from which students can choose and share comments with their group members in debriefing sessions. Reviewing their journals periodically during the entire semester will also give students feedback, in writing, as to the suitability of what is being learned.

This process will lead to discussions concerning any class trends that they have acknowledged through observation or from their journals. In addition, requiring all students to tender a final reflective report when a group project is completed can help them grasp the value of teamwork and the expertise they have cultivated through this procedure.

In conclusion, very different classroom environments have transpired as a result of diverse philosophical perspectives and psychological learning theories put forth by the educational administration and instructors. Some educators believe that knowledge is something created anew by each student and that learning will occur as a result of effort put forth on authentic tasks found in social environments and that the cognitive activities of these students resolves what they have learned.

If this is true, then the classroom should be one in which students work as groups/teams on assigned projects and discuss how best to solve problems as well as the meaning of the tasks to be achieved and the perception about what they are learning. Meanwhile, the teacher's role becomes one who facilitates learning by enabling students to make their own inquiries that are in association with their experience and takes control of their learning in order to make real-world applications.

Each educator sees the learning situation from a different perspective or point of view. Each individual student's past experiences will also affect their readiness to learn and the ability to comprehend the requirements involved in each circumstance encountered. The student can then react in accordance with how they view or feel about each situation. Most students have a fairly specific picture of what he or she wants to do and achieve. Therefore, learning has an active rationale in that, for students to learn, they need to react and respond both outwardly and inwardly with emotion and intellect in order for the learning process to change behavior.

SCL, in education, is an approach that focuses on student needs when the curriculum is designed on developing course content and on considering learning styles. Meanwhile, this process will create interest and interactivity that allow the instructor to become a facilitator of learning. As a method of learning, SCL acknowledges that the student is the central voice in the learning experience and requires students to become active by accepting responsibility for their own learning. Research by Armstrong (2012) indicated that traditional education ignores and suppresses the responsibility of the learner.

The object of SCL is to create hands-on and group/team work activities in which learners actively participate in the discovery process of learning while maintaining an autonomous point of view. In this process, students construct an innovative knowledge of the material to be learned in a creative environment. Advocates of SCL believe that through this process students can best achieve their lifelong learning goals, which will increase their motivation to learn.

Moreover, this learning process establishes individual behaviors of self-motivation, self-determination, and self-regulation. This process accommodates various learning styles that create the ability to accomplish educational objectives.

In order for this learning methodology to function efficiently, instructors must develop a constructivist-learning model that creates a student-centered learning atmosphere. For this learning procedure to be successful, students must be given the opportunity to discover their own learning style while being enabled to fully engage in an active learning process in which teachers make available learning routines that cater to specific student needs. Freestone (2012) states that traditional teaching is based on one learning style that focuses on content and is driven by the teacher.

Teacher-centered instruction generally involves one-way communication where students sit passively while listening. The teacher is viewed as the expert who imparts their knowledge on the subject matter being studied. Learning is then measured and evaluated via tests and exams in which scientific evidence designates that high grades on tests and examinations do not efficiently translate into student learning of material presented (Kraft 1978).

In contrast, student-centered education advocates that teachers and students focus better in a teaching and learning environment in which educators attempt to maximize student productivity, knowledge acquisition, skills augmentation, and personal development. Educators may use a variety of instructional devices and methods as well as flexible arrangements of time and place. Therefore, the learners assume primary responsibility for their choices and have opportunities to employ control over their learning. These efforts may often lead to collaborative partnerships among faculty, administration, staff, and the community at large.

This learner-centered environment makes possible the exploration of meaning and content knowledge through personal and interpersonal discovery. The process implies active commitment by the student and the assimilation of academics with the student's total development. Examples of SCL educational practices include, but are not limited to, collaborative group learning both inside and outside the classroom; individual student research and discovery develop problem-based, critical thinking, and inquiry learning. Braket (2005) noted that the move from traditional teaching to a student-centered approach requires the following five changes to occur:

- The balance of classroom authority must move from facilitator to students.
- The subject matter design must be built on knowledge rather than knowledge as an end in itself.
- The instructor must assume a position of facilitator and contributor of how knowledge is obtained rather than of administrator of knowledge.
- The responsibilities for learning must transfer from teacher to the learner in order to promote efficient and effective learning.

Student-centered learning methodology includes active-learning processes where students focus on problems to be solved and questions to be answered and formulate their own questions to be discussed, explained, and brainstormed in order to reach knowledgeable conclusions.

Additional information regarding assessment, group/teamwork, problem solving, independent and critical thinking can be found in appendix D.

Chapter Eight

Interactive Student Centered Learning (1)

THE PROCESS

Although there may be no universally accepted definition for interactive student centered learning, ISCL has been characterized as not being "traditional" or "chalk-and-talk" teaching. Information collected from educators indicates that ISCL occurs more frequently in National Certificate programs than in other teaching curriculums. In addition, there appears to be more progressive teaching/learning today than has been utilized in the past. About 95 percent of teaching staff members in colleges indicate that "nontraditional" methods form a significant part of their teaching, with nearly two-thirds saying that they, to a large extent, are using more progressive methods in their instruction.

A recent press release by the Los Angeles Unified School District tells of the institution of a new teaching curriculum that includes student-centered learning as a main approach to learning. Research has concluded that students do not learn much just sitting in class listening to teachers, memorizing prepackaged assignments, and spitting out the answers. Students must talk about what they are learning, write about it, relate it to past experiences, and apply it to their daily lives. Students must make what they learn part of themselves.

The major objective of ISCL is to develop a sense of inquiry, the desire to learn and to establish a "preferred environment" that creates a progressive learning atmosphere. Once this is achieved, students will learn to reason analytically and solve problems through critical thinking in order to develop concepts about the information or subject matter they want to learn.

There are several factors that must be cultivated if this approach to education is to occur: First, students must understand what they read and discuss and learn in order to apply this information to improve problem-solving and critical-thinking skills. Second, students must learn to use these skills creatively in order to condense/synthesize information and put this information into their own words, so it can be easily digested. Third, students must develop the ability to outline information into an organized format that is easily conceptualized. Last and maybe the most important is that they must develop the ability to communicate effectively.

The results will create students who are more creative, curious, and inventive. To achieve these results, students must learn to evaluate facts and make rational decisions while drawing reliable conclusions instead of basing decisions on personal emotions. To achieve this ability, students must develop two factors in making rational decisions: 1) deductive reasoning, or using the knowledge gained by reasoning to draw rational conclusions and 2) inductive reasoning, or reasoning from a particular instance to reach a general conclusion.

Students should understand that the process of learning is often more important than the subject matter to be learned and that they must be able to evaluate their own learning. Brainstorming is an important factor in ISCL. Often discussions are facilitated by presenting issues on a topic to be discussed and by forming a question that requires critical thinking and analytical reasoning to reach reasonable conclusions in which no value judgments are made regarding the answers. In addition, a forced-choice method of decision making can be used by calling upon students to take a side on an issue and defend their opinion.

The importance of developing and implementing this new approach to instruction and learning was stated during a conference on educational problems. Dr. Theodore Hershberg, a professor at the University of Pennsylvania, gave a talk, "Changing School Standards." It is Dr. Hershberg's thesis that we must raise the educational standard expected of each student if they are to compete in a global economy, improve classroom performance, and insure future employment after college. This insightful professor believes that this is best achieved through problem-solving instruction and effective instructional assessment.

With these comments in mind, the objective of ISCL is to establish a more positive, progressive classroom environment, through a problem-solving, critical-thinking and analytical reasoning approach to learning. A search of the Internet for information on student-centered learning and curriculum development led to an article by Judith Grunert, who stated "that there is drastic need for this type of process if instructional development is to improve learning." Dr. Clark, of the University of California, implied that no learning takes place without goals and problems to solve.

If this is true, then these methods of instruction and assessment are crucial for effective instruction and learning. The effectiveness of this method of learning was further driven home by a small pamphlet written by Dr. Paul Richards containing thirty practical ideas on how to improve student learning by developing problem-solving and critical-thinking skills.

In an order to make content more meaningful to students, class activities must be revised that stay relevant to the needs of student and keep the content as up-to-date as possible. To achieve this, articles from newspapers and magazines and other educational sources can be used as a means of making information and the concepts being taught more relevant as far as current research and trends are concerned.

LEARNING OBJECTIVES

An ISCL instructional format or strategy requires intense planning in order for classroom teaching to be effective. The objective is to determine the knowledge and skills that should result from the activities undertaken. Problem solving, critical thinking, comparing, and contrasting different points of view are specific tasks that create a well-planned method of organization. Analyzing problems to determine mistakes in their own learning seems to become a more personalized experience, which increases motivation by allowing students the opportunity to experiment and find solutions for themselves.

Interactive student-centered learning emphasizes active learning by encouraging students to ask questions and formulate their own hypotheses. This is a process of inquiry where the learner plays an important role in his or her learning. However, in order for ISCL to be successful, students must accept responsibility for learning in order for the process to change from instructor-centered to student-centered learning. Interactive student-centered learning is a form of learning by discovery in which students research the material to be learned on their own or in conjunction with other students and the instructor to determine what they need to know.

Throughout the process of problem solving, analytical reasoning, and critical thinking, individual students or student groups work at their own pace to search for information. Research indicates that in this format student learning is improved and students become more committed when they are actively involved in the learning process. This process has shown that it enhances student satisfaction with their learning experience, promotes self-esteem, and is more productive in comparison to the competitive learning experienced in the teacher lecture approach to learning.

Critical thinking, problem solving, and decision making play a significant role in educating students, and are important to achieving effective learning.

Critical thinking plays an essential role in the learning process in that it encompasses internalization of new ideas in conjunction with basic ideas, principles, and the concepts inherent in the content being studied. Critical thinking is also important in the application process of ideas, principles, and theories implemented and relevant to the learner's life and education.

Therefore, good teaching must cultivate critical thinking (often defined as *intellectually engaged thinking*) in the learning and educational processes. The key is for instructors to foster critical thinking and insightfulness in students by asking questions that stimulate constructive thinking important for developing knowledge since all students do their own learning.

In constructing knowledge, good teachers recognize and focus on activities that stimulate the students' minds into taking ownership of the key concepts and principles important to learning in that critical thinking utilizes logic and broad intellectual criteria that include clarity, credibility, accuracy, precision, relevance, and fairness in solving problems effectively.

Edward Glasser proposed that the following factors are important in thinking critically: 1) an attitude that considers, in a thoughtful way, the problems and subjects that come within the student's range of experiences; 2) a knowledge of the methods of logical inquiry and analytical reasoning; and 3) a skill in applying the methods of critical thinking that endures.

THE INSTRUCTOR'S ROLE

In ISCL the instructor's main effort is to develop a "preferred environment." In this system the instructor has three important responsibilities: first, the instructor must be an organizer of information and learning procedures; second, they must be a synthesizer that puts information into its simplest form: third, they must be a facilitator of information. As an organizer, the instructor establishes a systemic and structured learning environment. In ISCL teachers become organizers of knowledge rather than dispensers of information in which the major objective is to get students to change or modify their behavior.

An additional objective is to create inquiry/controversy discussion. The role of the instructor is not to impart knowledge but to create experiences in and out of the classroom in which learners are engaged in order to discover knowledge. In doing this, the learners find out for themselves what needs to be learned through participation and interaction in groups rather than having the teacher present them with the material to be learned. The result is that learning takes place at higher cognitive levels and increases student information retention.

Due to the reliance of students on the instructor to furnish them with information they need to know, students are often denied opportunities to develop the decision-making, self-monitoring, problem-solving skills necessary to optimize the learning experiences. The second role of the instructor is to synthesize (condense) information to be learned into its simplest form. In a difficult subject, the instructor assigning a textbook of over four hundred pages and requiring students to know everything in the book in addition to other assigned readings and projects is unrealistic.

Synthesis of information requires the instructor to fit the difficulty of the task to be learned to the skill and ability of the student and set realistic performance goals. Reducing the material to be learned into its simplest form enables all students to understand and relate it to the information being presented.

Synthesis enables students to outline material being studied and apply it to what they already know. With this basic understanding, students can now make reasonable decisions through discovery.

The third factor in the ISCL format of a preferred environment is that the instructor becomes a facilitator (a guide to learning) of information and assumes responsibility for developing optimal learning experiences that increase the student's ability to analyze, interpret, brainstorm, and solve problems in order to make informed decisions. In addition, it provides affective objectives that change student attitudes and increases student motivation while encouraging responsibility.

As a facilitator of knowledge, the instructor's responsibility is to provide the tools and information needed to solve problems and learn concepts in order for the learner to make sense of what is to be learned and reach responsible conclusions. In this process, students become less dependent on receiving knowledge from teachers and accepting predetermined conclusions of others. Students learn by collecting and organizing information that enables them to reach their own conclusions through analysis, synthesis, and evaluation.

This process allows students to ascertain information and ideas on their own or within a group, which is the most natural way to learn and makes the information and concepts to be learned and remembered easier while keeping everyone active.

Teachers reported significant increases in the use of teaching methods that involved students actively in their learning process. Group work, practical work, projects and assignments, simulations and role play are all being used more than ever before. Most teachers now allow students to progress at their own pace. Over 60 percent of teachers surveyed indicate that they have reduced the use of the "whole-class" teacher-centered procedures.

Disadvantages

Some of the complaints regarding ISCL are similar to those put forth by educators discussed in previous chapters. At this stage, it must be pointed out to students and instructors that there are some weaknesses in the ISCL method of teaching. Often it is difficult to get some students to fully participate because the process is often time-consuming. In addition, it is difficult to cover significant amounts of content and requires extreme preparation by instructor and students.

One of the things that disturbs some instructors is that they have less control of the learning process. In addition, some the students often do not relate well to ISCL due to the inability to work in groups and that the transition from traditional to student-centered learning is difficult and time-consuming.

On the whole, teachers welcome the changes in teaching that have taken place; students also indicate they appreciate the new emphasis on practical work, projects, assignments, and diagnostic assessment. National Certificate schools have been successful in encouraging more adventurous teaching, but that is not the whole story. It became apparent that what the teachers valued less were the teaching methods they used the most and now appreciate the freedom they have to extend their repertoire and increase the range of techniques used. Variety is the key word to successful teaching and learning.

Some teachers wished to abandon "chalk-and-talk" altogether, since its role is being redefined it is no longer seen as the sole method of teaching. However, good teaching is about humor that is often self-deprecating. A show of humor indicates that the instructor is not taking him- or herself too seriously; that makes their presentations more acceptable and helps develop credibility. By not maintaining a fixed agenda, the instructor remains flexible and fluid in reacting to the daily changing circumstances in classroom procedures. While some teachers welcomed student-centered learning wholeheartedly, others identified factors preventing its full use.

Chief among these factors were time and resources. Comments such as "student-centered learning is the most effective approach, but is very difficult to implement in the time allowed for a teaching unit," was a common statement. Some educators further stated that it is difficult for them to give individual schooling to a group of students in that it was too time-consuming. These teachers found that a few minutes spent showing something on the board can save an awful lot of time.

Teachers were also reluctant to commit themselves completely to student-centered learning because they felt that some of their students were not ready to take on this responsibility because they experience difficulty in not always being able to work with others to discover information. There was some evidence from students that they were not fully aware of their own learning processes and, therefore, could not take full advantage of ISCL techniques.

Benefits

Given the importance of attitudes and capabilities for lifelong learning, students have to accept greater responsibility for their own learning. This is inherent in any ISCL approach to learning and has made an important step in education and intellectual development. Faculty members can now work with students to elevate deeper questions about how they learn and what adjustment they can make that will facilitate their own learning.

The openness of ISCL provides students with the opportunity for developing or using their own learning style while instituting this most important knowledge-producing process. Student-centered learning has carryover benefits for both the student and instructor. Students not only improve learning and other skills but also gain knowledge and abilities that will follow them throughout their lifetime. Students learn the relationship between what they are responsible for or not responsible for and also their rights as students, while learning becomes fun for both the instructor and student.

The following is a brief list of several key benefits of ISCL suggested by Kornell and Bjork (2007) that will assist learners in taking control of their own learning in order to make accurate determinations of how they learn.

- It strengthens student motivation.
- It promotes effective communication skills.
- It reduces disruptive behavior in groups and classrooms.
- It advances discovery and active learning.
- Students must take responsibility for their own learning.
- The facilitator can now employ several new and effective teaching methods.
- The focal point is directed to what the student does instead of teacher presentations.
- Focus is mainly transferred to the process of learning.
- A variety of assessment procedures are used as a part of the learning process.
- It creates the opportunity for students to explore their own learning styles.

ASSESSMENT-EVALUATION

Although reviewed in the earlier student teaching methods presented, assessment will be discussed here briefly. In education, assessment is the analysis/measurement of what is to be achieved and how it is to be implemented. The instructor will want to expand ways to assess the process of determining student performance, as well as the product of their learning. Assessment in ISCL is not determined by just taking a test at the end of a unit. It has been determined by experts that in evaluating learning there are three elements of the learning procedure that include content, the process, and product development.

It is a performance-based, faultless, generative, and ongoing procedure that presents students with multiple essential opportunities to demonstrate what they have learned. Students and instructors must have written goals and objectives of what is to be learned in addition to the development of well-written and defined assignments to be achieved and assessed.

Research indicates that assessment and evaluation affects what students learn and provides the tools needed to measure how well the students achieved the outcomes learning. This process is based on what the instructor wants the students to know and be able to do as a result of their increase in knowledge.

The question to be asked is: Did the assigned assessments take into account prior student knowledge and what they were trying to learn as a result of the continuous process that occurs throughout the learning cycle? This should include the three ways of assessing the learning process as well as a final project. Other questions to ask are: Were students able to overcome the challenge brought forth by the learning process? Were students thoroughly involved in learning by doing? And were they able to communicate what they had learned to others and the facilitator?

Evaluation is taking the information that has been assessed and verifying, judging, and classifying individual and group performance and achievement. As teaching shifts from traditional learning to ISCL, the students must assume full responsibility for their level of involvement and participation necessary for assessing their learning goals and evaluating what they learned.

The following are issues from several studies that should be incorporated into evaluation in the assessment process:

- Were relationships established among group members equally and did this support student learning?
- Did assessment measure personal improvement?
- Did students complete their daily journals?
- Were peer and self-assessment Included?
- Was equal participation cultivated during projects and group work, which improved individual skills and knowledge competencies?
- Did the assessment tools take into account whether learners were engaged in real-world tasks or applications?
- Did assessment enable students to achieve equal performance opportunities?

- Did the assessment allow students to use higher level thinking and problem-solving skills?
- Was a formula created to evaluate the students' progress throughout the assigned undertaking?
- Were students allowed to assist in developing goals and standards for the evaluation each task performed?
- Was previous knowledge and experiences taken into account?
- Was the accumulated information valuable to the learner and instructor and significant to curriculum development?

Evaluation is the process of determining what the collected data means to the student, teacher, and curriculum. In order to get the best student achievement results the teacher must know what and when to re-teach and when to further challenge the students. While evaluating the results of the student's performance did assessment guide the direction and focuses of new curriculum design for revising projected content? In short, evaluation is what students and instructors do with the assessed material they have collected throughout the project/class.

Once the teacher has studied the results of assessment and evaluation a point of view regarding content, process, and product should be established. Having confirmed a concept of what each process is trying to introduce, the instructors will understand how the goals, standards, and eventual outcomes begin to fit together. After the teacher has studied the significant components of assessment and evaluation, judgments regarding content, process, and product can be established that are reasonable.

STUDENT GROUP PARTICIPATION

Interactive student-centered learning is a formal instructional approach that allows students to work individually and together in small groups (teams) to accomplish common goals in classroom study groups consisting of students with varying ethic and social differences, mental skills, and leadership abilities. These groups are committed to achieving common goals and solving problems that ether they or the instructor find to be important. Well-designed group assignments give students specific responsibilities for creating effective group activities and setting instructional guidelines that describe how students should work together.

Students in each group should be given critical thinking exercises consisting of questions that require in-depth thought, brainstorming, and analytical reasoning to solve the problems posed. As a result of shared knowledge and good leadership, groups will improve their communication and independent thinking skills as they become responsible and accountable for working on their decision making in cooperation with other members of the group. In addition, independent-thinking students become responsible and accountable for working with others in order to accomplish the learning tasks assigned by the instructor.

Through this learning process, students begin to understand that cooperative effort by all members of the group result in mutual benefits for all members. Group and individual student accountability and assessments are easier to achieve if groups are kept small (four to five students in each group). Evaluating student and group progress can be accomplished by randomly calling on individual students in a group to explain the information being studied. Participation in group work can be evaluated by having a student checker rate each student's participation and contribution to the group.

Discussion assignments by individual groups should begin by asking questions such as: What problem is the group/team trying to solve? What are the similarities between the various parts of the questions? What solutions, answers, or conclusion can be made? Next, the groups need to decide what steps are called for to solve the problems presented, what approach should be used in researching the problems, and finally what each member's responsibility is.

The last decision to be made is to determine what resources should be used by the group/team to research the problem. Several places to start their research would be the Internet, knowledgeable staff members, text/slides/videos, textbooks, and other resources made available by the library and instructor.

Once each group has completed their investigation, they meet in the classroom to discuss the results of their research and how the results of their study should be presented to the whole class. Although only certain questions are assigned to each group for presentation to the class, each group is responsible for having briefly studied and answered all questions in order to stimulate class discussion. Individual students in each group are assigned topics to research and present first to their group for discussion. Once these group discussions have concluded, class discussion can take place.

All in-class group meetings are conducted under the supervision of the instructor who meets with each group prior to class discussions to validate each question and review how assigned questions will be presented to the class. At this time the instructor answers any question or problems the group may have regarding their research and class presentations.

Once the learning tasks to be accomplished have been determined, each individual member of the group will be held accountable for completion of the problems assigned. Likewise, assignment results can be achieved by simply randomly calling on group members to present the group's solution to the question or problems presented. Assessment can be made more encompassing by requiring both peer assessment and feedback

KEY IDEAS TO REMEMBER

Interactive student-centered learning creates a preferred environment that considers the needs, desires, and interests of the students while making the learning experience both fun and enjoyable. The first step is to develop organizational procedures and establish a means for students to present assignment to the class. This process produces objectives that enable students to change or modify behavior. In this undertaking, learning becomes an active, instead of a passive, process as the procedures and the process of learning become as important as the content being studied.

The end result of ISCL is the developments of students who are more creative, curious, and inventive while learning to evaluate facts and make rational decisions that allow them to draw reliable conclusions. This can be achieved by cultivating the ability to:

- reason analytically to solve problems and develop new concepts;
- condense-synthesize information;
- put what they have learned into their own word and thoughts
- develop a sense of inquiry and the desire to learn;
- outline information into an organized format;
- do a root-cause analysis by identifying the cause of the problem
- develop the ability to listen and communicate effectively;
- use a trial-and-error method by testing possible solutions until the right one is found
- divide and conquer the problems by breaking down a large, complex problem into s smaller, solvable problems.

Different classroom environments occur as a result of diverse philosophical outlooks and psychological learning theories put forth by educational administrators and instructors. Progressive educators believe that knowledge is something created anew by each student, and learning occurs as a result of working on authentic tasks in a social situation that requires mental activities of each student in order to determine what he or she has learned. If this is true, classes should be composed of students working individually and as a group or team on assigned projects.

Students should be able to discuss how best to solve problems that arise and advance the importance of regarding each task allocated by cultivating concepts about what they have learned. Interactive student-centered learning is a form of learning by discovery in which students research the material to be learned on their own or in conjunction with other students to determine what they need to know through the process of analytical reasoning and critical thinking. Individual students and/or student groups work at their own pace to research the problems to be solved.

Research indicates that in this student-learning format, knowledge is improved while students become more committed to this learning process. Instructors must understand that in ISCL each individual student's past environmental circumstances will affect their readiness to learn and how they will react to and comprehend each situation encountered. Interactive student-centered learning emphasizes active earning by encouraging the learners to ask questions and formulate their own hypotheses.

Student-centered learning (SCL) is a combination of all the methods of learning discussed above that places emphasis on interactive learning. Inductive teaching and learning is a process in which students are presented with questions and problems that challenge their learning of course material in a context that challenges students through project-based and learning by discovery principles. Additional information on problem solving, critical thinking, group/teamwork and assessment can be found in appendix D.

Chapter Nine

Interactive Student Centered Learning (2)

INSTRUCTIONAL DEVELOPMENT

After the instructor and/or the administration has decided to institute a student-centered learning itinerary, the next step is to develop the methods, structure, organization, and other factors necessary for an efficient and effective instructional plan. The objective of any instructional plan is to be sure students are thoroughly informed of course expectations, requirements, organizational procedures, and so on.

In order to be successful, students need to know how to function so that their efforts are productive and they accomplish assigned tasks successfully and efficiently. The main objective of chapter 8 is to outline the factors that establish an effective instructional process plan.

Therefore, the objective of this section of ISCL is to inform instructors and interested administrators how the instructional process of ISCL can be developed and operated by providing a program outline that, with minor adjustments, can be used to teach almost any subject and level of education. This program and system was used in teaching U.S. history, lifetime wellness, and public speaking courses at every level of education from secondary to community college and university levels.

The students were always receptive and very cooperative in what the program was trying to achieve, and student performance improved immensely. Once the instructor has determined what the students need to learn and selected a textbook, purchased a handbook, and other course material, instructional management strategies must be developed that outline the content, structure, and other factors needed to institute an ISCL course of action.

ISCL emphasizes active learning by encouraging students to ask questions and formulate their own hypotheses. This is a process of inquiry where the learners and groups play an important role in how each student is learning.

However, in order for ISCL to be successful, students must accept responsibility and accountability for their learning, and that will enable the process to change from instructor-centered to student-centered learning. ISCL is a form of learning by discovery in which students research the material to be learned on their own or in conjunction with others to determine what they need to know and how to acquire that knowledge. Through the process of problem solving, analytical reasoning, and critical thinking, individual students and student group/teams work at their own pace to search for information.

Research indicates that in this format student learning is improved, and students become more committed when they are actively involved in learning. This process has also been shown to enhance student satisfaction with their learning experience and promote self-esteem and is more productive than the competitive learning experienced in the teacher-centered learning approach. A major factor in ISCL is problem-based learning PBL that connects practice and theory in order to engage students in solving real-life problems that they face daily. Only through the process of analysis, application, and evaluation can an increased level of skill be achieved that creates a more active approach to learning.

This problem-solving process will motivate students to gain knowledge in a real world approach to learning situations. Due to the lack of structure, PBL is thought of as a risky educational process. This criticism is irrelevant in that the process is a byproduct of problem solving that has many ways of resolving or reaching a solution to the problems that need to be solved.

Therefore, the underlying belief of PBL is the creation of learning environments that are more meaningful and fun when self-directed small active groups are activated. As a result, this process encourages students to take responsibility for their own and group learning. In problem-solving learning, the faculty becomes engaged in coaching and critiquing the process as it takes place in order to control the volume of information being delivered.

The research of Savoie and Hughes (1994) outlines six steps that best organize PBL classroom experiences:

- Begin with a problem.
- Make sure the problems presented relate to the student's world.
- The subject matter should be organized around the problem, not the discipline.
- Students should be given the major responsibility of determining and directing the learning process.

- The class must involve small groups of only five to six students.
- Students must be able to demonstrate what they have learned by producing a product or presenting a project.

The great aspect of PBL is that students construct knowledge based on knowledge previously learned (Cross 1998). The problem-solving process works best if students answer the following questions: 1) What do they know? 2) What do they need to know? 3) What are they going to do to solve the problem/s?

Commencing with the organization of classroom instruction and presentations based on an ISCL approach to learning requires the development of a student handbook that contains a syllabus and workbook that includes course content and other class assignments. This handbook also provides students with a tentative course outline, class assignments, course requirement, grading procedures, and other material that creates an effective and efficient learning environment. The objective is to provide students with guidelines such as setting an agenda, specifying time limits, developing procedures, and monitoring how the agenda is progressing. The content and organization of a handbook can be found in chapter 10.

These and other features can be placed on an Internet web page that establishes a forum for informing students of changes in course expectations, assignments, and other organizational factors. Below is an outline of the features required when designing an ISCL course.

INSTRUCTIONAL MANAGEMENT

This section consists of items that allow instructors to micro-manage student behavior while assigning them the responsibility of understanding class procedures and other information pertinent to effective instructional management. A complete knowledge of each of the factors will be reviewed as this project unfolds. The following are features that build effective and efficient instructional management:

1. Provide a complete explanation of student responsibilities, requirements, and instructional management procedures that should take place.
2. Establish student learning resources including a textbook, handbook, syllabus, workbook, and other sources for procuring information.
3. A daily attendance form for recording absence and other pertinent attendance information should be made available.
4. A copy of each student's daily schedule is created.

5. Provide a weekly schedule outlining specific, in-class and group, activities to be achieved each day during class session.
6. Confirm classroom structure and arrangements.
7. Establish group/team size, responsibilities, and personnel.
8. Determine the media to be procured and used.
9. Ascertain the factors that are to be used in assessment and evaluation of student performance.
10. Copies of student projects and assignment must be allocated.
11. Learning goals must be developed by each student, group, and class.

INSTRUCTIONAL STRATEGIES

1. **Case Based Learning/Teaching Methods:** This approach to learning and teaching utilizes real or imagined scenarios that teach students about their field of study (Barnes 1994).
2. **Concept Mapping:** This is a graphic representation for organizing and representing the pieces and parts of knowledge (Bloom 1956).
3. **Discussion Questions:** Engage students by challenging them to think by analyzing, synthesizing, and evaluating the subject matter.
4. **Peer Teaching:** This is a collaborative-learning and peer teaching method that is a student-centered process that encourages student involvement, discovery, manipulation, and personal research of information (Hebert 1998).

Instructor's Role

The major factor in developing an ISCL format is the process of developing a preferred environment in which the instructor becomes a facilitator (a guide to acquiring information and achieving knowledge) while assuming responsibility for developing optimal learning experiences that increase each student's learning and expertise. In addition, the instructor provides affective objectives that change each student's attitude and behavior and that increase student motivation while encouraging responsibility.

As a facilitator of knowledge, the instructor is accountable for providing the tools and information needed to analyze, interpret, and solve problems, while developing learning concepts that make it possible for the students to make sense out of what is to be learned and reach responsible conclusions. In this course of action, students become less dependent on receiving knowledge from teachers and accepting predetermined conclusions of others.

Students learn by collecting and organizing information that enables them to reach their own conclusions through analysis, synthesis, and evaluation. This process allows students to actively ascertain information and ideas on their own (with minimal facilitator assistance), which is the most natural way to learn the information and make concepts easier to remember.

HANDBOOK

The handbook is an instruction manual that contains information regarding features that provide the procedures and learning materials needed by the student to complete course requirements. These items include the textbook and other reading materials that are to be used and a syllabus. The syllabus contains a workbook containing class assignments that provide the basic responsibilities required of each student. To achieve these basic resources, students need only refer to the handbook for this information. Several student information forms that each student must fill out and return to the instructor by the next class meeting are also included.

These forms state that the student understands their responsibilities and class requirements. In addition, each student signs activity and class-procedure contracts that spell out the student requirements, class organization, and grading procedures. Also included is a section called "Tools for Learning," which helps students in developing learning and knowledge that will assist in achieving academic success. The handbook will be covered in depth in appendix A.

Classroom Procedures

Students are informed of course expectations and a complete review of the handbook; syllabus and workbook are discussed in class. Included in appendix B is a syllabus containing a tentative course outline, class assignments, course requirement, grading procedures, and other materials The syllabus and workbook will create an effective and efficient learning environment based on the understanding that students will know in advance where the class is heading, what is required of them to meet the mandatory standards that have been established, and when assignments are due. This information is discussed in great detail during the first week of class and reviewed periodically throughout the semester. Each student needs only to refer to the workbook for essential information. Several student-information forms are included for students to fill out and return to the instructor that states they understand the responsibilities, requirements, and course of study.

In addition, each student signs an activity and class-procedure contract that spells out the requirements of class organization and grading procedures. In order to make course content more meaningful to students, class activities are undertaken that are relevant to the needs and interests of the student by keeping the content as up-to-date as possible.

Multimedia

New technology can be used to produce PowerPoint presentations for each of the units taught in a course. The slides can contain cartoons, stories, examples, music, and illustrations, etc., that move and make sounds to make learning fun and interesting while relating to various learning styles. The objective of these presentations is to present the material to be learned in an audio and visual format that catches and maintains the student's attention and concentration.

The PowerPoint slides contain an introduction to content being studied and the objective to be reached. The slides can also contain important quotes and critical-thinking activities for brainstorming the groups' and class's discussion questions. Also included are problem-solving questions that require research, analytical reasoning, and critical thinking to answer. These activities when completed are discussed in small groups and then as a class activity. In several units music (songs) can be used to emphasize what the writer is trying to say regarding the subject being studied. These questions are then discussed in groups and answers are presented to the whole class.

These materials are also a great way to provide data to visually skilled learners and reinforce facts and information being covered. This process makes the class environment more acceptable and helps develop credibility. By not maintaining a fixed agenda and remaining flexible and fluid in reacting to daily changing circumstances in the classroom creates an efficient and effective class and study atmosphere. As previously mentioned, ISCL emphasizes active learning by encouraging learners to ask question and formulate their own hypotheses.

Assessment/Evaluation

Assessment of student activities is used to evaluate student performance in classroom studies and group performance. Literature based on student-centered learning concludes that assessment as an appraisal of student progress and evaluation is the value (grade) given for student performance. The question instructors must ask themselves is: Does the end result of evaluations clearly match the content being assessed with accurate measurements? Following are several areas that the evaluator must consider when assessing and evaluating performance and assigning a grade.

- The first item the instructor must consider when grading performance is whether the individual student and his or her team achieved the goals set for them and the group.
- Second is how well each student performed in team activities.

- Third, student performance in oral discussions, projects, and written reports are evaluated.
- Fourth is the comparison of pre-exams with final or exit exams.
- The fifth deals with student classroom behavior and discussion performance.
- Sixth is based on attendance.
- Seventh, students make a personal evaluation of their own and group overall performance.
- Eighth, did students achieve the goals they set for themselves or their group?

In the classroom the skills to be evaluated are the ability to use critical thinking and problem solving to analyze the data being researched and their presentations of this data to the group and class, in addition to course content information and knowledge accomplished. Students evaluate their own learning in some situations, which is determined by how they displayed the required factors being evaluated.

TEAM/GROUP PARTICIPATION

ISCL is a formal instructional approach that allows students to work individually and together in small groups (teams) to accomplish common goals. Each small group should be assembled with students of diverse skills and ethnic backgrounds. These groups are committed to achieving common goals and solve problems that either they or the instructor find important. Well-designed group assignments give students a specific task for creating effective group activities and setting instructional guidelines that describe how students should work together.

Students in each group are given critical-thinking exercises consisting of questions that require in-depth thought and analytical reasoning to solve the problems proposed. As a result of shared knowledge, groups improve leadership, communication, and decision-making skills, in cooperation with other members within the group. In addition to independent thinking, students become responsible and accountable for working with others in order to accomplish the learning tasks assigned by the instructor.

As a result, students begin to understand that collaborative and cooperative efforts by all members of the group results in mutual benefits for all members. Students should be provided with guidelines for moving forward in meetings, such as how to set and follow an agenda, specific time of group meeting, and how to monitor progress. Some means for developing conflict resolution should also be established by creating a group contract that spells out the various rules and responsibilities of each member.

In addition, students must create effective methods of giving and receiving feedback. Furthermore, the group must determine the role that suits each student best. However, rotating student roles will expand individual student skills. Group and individual student accountability and assessments are easier to achieve if groups remain small (four to five students in each group). Evaluating student and group progress can be accomplished by randomly calling on individual students, in a group, to explain the information being studied. Involvement in group work can also be realized by having a student checker rate each student's participation and contribution to the group.

Discussion assignments instituted by individual groups should begin by asking questions such as: What are the problem/s we are trying to solve? What is the relation between the various parts of the questions? What solutions, answers, or conclusion can be made? Next, the groups need to determine what steps are needed to solve the problems presented, what methods should be used in researching the problems, and finally what each member's responsibility is. The last decision to be made is to determine what resources should be used in researching the problems presented. Several places to start research would be the Internet, knowledgeable staff members, the text, slides/videos, or other resources available to the student.

Once the groups have completed their research, they meet in the classroom to discuss the results of their research as a group and how these results should be presented to the class as a whole. Although only certain questions are assigned to each group member for presentation to the class, each group member is responsible for having researched all questions.

In order to stimulate discussion, individual students in each group are assigned a topic or topics to research, so that they can be presented and discussed in their group. Once these discussions have concluded, members of each group are appointed to present the conclusions of their assigned questions to the group and finally to the class as a whole for further discussion.

All in class group meetings are conducted under the supervision of the instructor who meets with each group prior to class presentation, to review the correctness of each assigned question and how the assigned questions will be presented to the entire class. At this time the instructor deals with any question or problems the group may have regarding research and class presentation. Once the learning tasks to be accomplished are determined, each individual member of a group is held accountable for completion of the problem/s assigned. Assessment results can be achieved by simply grading each group member's presentation of their solutions to the question or problems presented.

Assessment of group presentations can become less complex by requiring peer assessment and/or student feedback regarding each student's performance. All group activities should be designed to build a strong interdependence that encourages members to help each other. This will motivate and encourage the less prepared members to work harder. Furthermore, one of the most important events a facilitator can accomplish is to have students reflect regularly on their group experiences, which will improve teamwork expertise.

KEY IDEAS TO REMEMBER

The interactive student-centered learning/teaching method requires that students work individually in interactive groups and in conjunction with the instructor/facilitator. This student-centered learning process shifts the focus of learning and summarizes the major learning methodologies. Student-centered methodologies have repeatedly shown to be better methods of learning than the traditional learning/instructional approach and improve both short-term as well as long-term retention and an in-depth understanding of course material.

In addition, there is an increased ability to think critically while developing creative problem-solving skills. This learning process forms positive attitudes toward learning the topics being taught and a higher confidence in the process of acquiring knowledge and learning skills.

Chapter Ten

Interactive Student Centered Learning (3)

PROGRAM DEVELOPMENT

The purpose for including a program development handbook (appendix A) and workbook (appendix C) in this book is to make available information and data to prospective instructors or administrators that outline a student-centered learning curriculum, which includes several methods of approaching ISCL. The learning methodologies proposed here have been successfully used in teaching lifetime wellness, U.S. History, and public speaking classes at several levels of teaching. The information included in the appendixes includes the handbook, a syllabus (appendix B) and the workbook, which are samples of data used in the teaching and grading of the above course and can be restructured to fit almost any subject being studied.

In keeping with what this book is trying to achieve, these course curricula and teaching methodologies were developed and based on an interactive student-centered learning process that also includes cooperative, collaborative, and constructive approaches to students' education. As proposed throughout this manuscript, the instructor becomes a facilitator, organizer, and synthesizer in addition to being a dispenser of information and knowledge. This instructional process is based on developing analytical reasoning, problem solving, and critical thinking skills by presenting students with problems to solve, questions to answer, and concepts to be understood that make the course assignment student centered rather than text or lecture centered

This process requires students to assume responsibility for seeing that all assignments are completed on time as mandated by the facilitator. The course content is designed to meet the individual needs of each student while the problems, questions, and issues presented are the point of entry into the subject matter and are motivational tools for sustained inquiry and effort. It is hoped that the activities undertaken in this component of the manuscript will help instructors in establishing an ISCL approach to learning as well as teaching. In addition, students will learn the importance of discipline and have the capacity for lifelong learning as well as gain subject matter knowledge.

Course subject matter is assignment centered requiring students to formulate ideas and concepts both independently and with collaborative efforts of small groups and the class in problem-solving activities. The course procedures include activities outside the classroom that include library visitations and other areas of research needed to complete the projects and other assignments in a timely fashion. Students are expected to read the assigned chapters in the text and complete the assigned labs at the end of each chapter. Students individually and in their assigned groups will also complete corresponding units in the student handbook. Class activities include the following assignments:

- introductory information presented by the facilitator;
- brainstorming and critical thinking activities;
- chapter reviews;
- video and PowerPoint presentation discussions;
- assigned text discussion questions
- student individual oral reports and group panel discussions, etc.

Students who have taken courses based on ISCL often voiced that the information presented in the handbook gave them a good idea, in advance, of where the class was heading, what was required of them to meet the established standards, and when work was due. Several information forms were included in the syllabus for student to fill out and sign, indicating that they understood their responsibilities and class requirements.

The handbook was developed to provide students with a syllabus and workbook based on an ISCL perspective. The objective of the handbook is to construct basic course organization, requirements, and content that is more meaningful to the student. The basic idea is to assemble class activities relevant to each student's needs and keep the content as up-to-date and as fun as possible. The syllabus contains a tentative course outline, assignments, and course requirements in addition to assessment, evaluation, and grading procedures and other material needed to create an effective and efficient learning environment.

This information is discussed in great detail during the first week of class and reviewed periodically throughout the quarter/semester. Each student needs only to refer to the handbook and workbook for this information.

Several student information forms are also included that students are required to fill out and return to the instructor. In signing these forms, the student states that they fully understand their responsibilities and the requirements of the course.

In addition, each student signs activity and class procedure contracts that spell out the requirements of class organization and grading procedures. Chapter 8 contains in-depth data and information regarding the teacher's role and student assessment.

However, having established strict requirements and fixed agendas the classes remain flexible and fluid in reacting to the changing circumstances that occur in the classroom. The first section in the handbook contains a syllabus used to introduce students to the class procedures and provides advice that directs students in how to succeed in an unfamiliar and established educational procedure. The main objective of the syllabus is to inform students regarding what they need to know and do in order to achieve a high level of success.

Included are data on how the class operates and is structured as well as student responsibilities. The syllabus begins with an introduction to the concepts and factors included in this book. Also included is a letter to the student introducing the program, followed by a section on how to use the syllabus to get the most out of their efforts in the class.

Important information about the teacher and course description is provided in addition to how to contact the instructor as well as information about the class composition. There are several pages that outline a tentative calendar of events to be studied that includes the order of events and the chapter in the book that pertains to the course requirements that must be studied and understood.

Next, is the factor that students are most interested in, which include assessment, evaluations, and grading procedures. This includes how grades are achieved and the process of determining student evaluation. Although not included here, there is a handout given directly to a student that allows them to assess and grade the instructor as to his or her performance. Two pages are dedicated to a student contract that the student must read, sign, and return to the instructor. "Learning Tools" is a section that includes information about how students learn. Also included are sections on study skills, how to study for exams, and how best to communicate with other students and the instructor.

Also included is information that provides students with the best way to study for learning to take place. Finally, suggestions on how to write a paper and give an oral report are made available for students to review. The objective of ICSL is to make course content more meaningful to students, and it endeavors to make class activities relevant to their needs while keeping the content as simple and up-to-date as possible.

Chapter 10

KEYS TO REMEMBER

As previously stated, cartoons, stories, examples, and illustrations in PowerPoint are used to make the course fun and interesting. The objective of these features is to create an effective and efficient learning environment so that students know in advance where the class is heading, what is required of them to meet the standards that have been established, and when work is due.

Once again, this information is discussed in great detail during the first week of class and reviewed periodically throughout the quarter or semester and reinforced in a tentative course outline. A major factor in the development of ICSL is the establishment of a "preferred environment" in which the instructor becomes a facilitator (a guide to learning) of information and assumes responsibility for developing optimal learning experiences that increase the student's ability to analyze, interpret, and solve problems in order to make informed decisions.

In addition, this learning process provides affective objectives that change student attitudes and increase student motivation while encouraging responsibility. Brainstorming in open discussion is facilitated by presenting issues on the subject/s being studied in the form of questions that require analytical reasoning and critical thinking to reach responsible conclusions in which value judgments are made regarding how they are answered. A preferred environment develops a sense of inquiry and the desire to learn. This process also allows students to condense and synthesize information by putting it into their own words so they understand what they have read and have the ability to apply it.

Appendix A contains a student handbook that outlines the factors that establish a course of study and that will aid the instructor in developing an ISCL approach to learning and teaching. It is based on teaching the lifetime wellness course but can be adapted to conform to almost any discipline or subject taught at the college or secondary level. This educational process was used by the author in teaching lifetime wellness, United States History, and public speaking courses. This teaching and learning was extremely successful in student development and enlightened students as to their responsibility in the learning process. Some of the factors included in the handbook are:

- information regarding class procedures/student contracts;
- course description;
- student responsibility;
- student contract;
- various learning aids;
- study skills;
- goal development;
- purpose of course

- curriculum objective.

Appendix A

Student Handbook

INSTRUCTOR'S INFORMATION

INSTRUCTOR: Name

OFFICE:

OFFICE HOURS: 1:05 – 2:00 PM

COURSE TITLE: Lifetime Wellness

REQUIRED TEXT: *Physical Fitness and Wellness*, Jerrod S. Greenberg

DEPARTMENTS: Physical Education, Lifetime Wellness, History, Public Speaking

PHONE:
Office_____
Home_____

CLASS TIME: MTWT 9:00–10:00/ MW 5:30–7:10 pm

COURSE NUMBER: PEH 100

LETTER TO STUDENTS

It is the instructor's greatest desire that students enjoy this course. For most of you it is an elective course, but a very special course that could have everlasting effects on your longevity and ability to perform the daily chores of life. I personally feel that it may be the most valuable course taught that students will take during their college career because it deals with their personal fitness, health, and well-being that will be with students for a lifetime. It will not be an easy course, due to time constraints and the abundance of material to be covered.

However, every issue taken up in this course is of fundamental importance to living and developing a broad view of the elements important to living a satisfactory wellness lifestyle. Extending the effort required and fighting through the difficulties will reward students with the insights and perspectives that will lead to success in school and life.

This course is designed to accomplish two important tasks: (1) to introduce students to the theories, concepts, and knowledge needed to achieve a wellness lifestyle, while reviewing positions on current issues in health, wellness, and nutrition, and (2) to provide quality time to improve your aerobic and anaerobic fitness as well as flexibility. Therefore, the first goal is to develop the ability to make responsible decisions about wellness and fitness, and second, to put these decisions into practice. The difficulty is that the major responsibility for meeting course requirements is one that students must assume.

If students accept and attend to these responsibilities with care, they will be successful in this course while preparing their body and mind in a positive fashion. A side benefit of the course is that students will learn to accept the responsibility for their success in addition to learning and understanding important information about wellness and fitness. Furthermore, as students wrestle with the vast unfamiliar vocabulary and concepts that will strengthen their own vocabulary and knowledge, they will gain access to information that will improve their chances for success in real life's struggles.

The first section of the syllabus is designed to be an introduction to the class and provide information that will help students succeed in this class. It has also been designed to provide information about the responsibilities and assignments necessary to optimize students' ability to succeed. The second section contains tools for learning that will increase their chances for success in whatever endeavors they intend to participate. In preparing for life's endeavors, school has two objectives. The first objective is to provide students with a formal education so they can compete and perform more effectively in the outside world.

The second objective is to develop social skills that include developing efficient communication skills needed to further social relationships. Although both of these factors are important to functioning productively in society, the main emphasis of education is to develop expertise in a student's chosen areas of study. Therefore, 75 percent or more of a student's school time must be spent in activities that will increase knowledge in those areas. It has been determined by experts in the field of learning that for every hour spent in classroom activities, three hours must be spent outside of class in study and preparation.

Therefore, if students are in class for 9 hours per week, approximately 27 hours should be spent in preparation. This means that about 50 percent of the hours available to the student per week must be spent in activities related to classroom success. So plan thoroughly and use your time wisely. Good luck

COURSE DESCRIPTION

This course is a learning-centered interactive approach to the study of wellness. Your instructor will be an organizer, synthesizer, and facilitator as well as a dispenser of information. Brainstorming and critical thinking presents students with problems, questions, and concepts that make the course assignment-centered rather than text or lecture centered, which is an important aspect of this course. It is the student's responsibility to see that all assignments are completed on time and as required. Course content is designed to meet the individual and group needs of each student. Problems, questions, and issues are the point of entry into the subject matter and a motivational tool for sustained inquiry and effort.

It is hoped that the activities undertaken in the course will help students learn the importance of discipline and the capacity for lifelong learning as well as subject matter knowledge. Course subject matter is assignment centered, requiring students to formulate their ideas and concepts both independently and in collaborative small groups that contain problems-solving activities.

Course procedures include classroom activities twice per week and fitness activities in the gym twice a week. Students are expected to read the assigned chapters in the text and complete lab assignments at the end of each chapter. Students will also complete corresponding units in the student workbook. Classroom activities include the following:

- Chapter lecture review and brief introductory evaluations
- Lecture/Discussions of group problem-solving discussion questions
- Student individual reports and group panels
- PowerPoint presentations and videos that cover activities being studied

Physical fitness activities take place twice a week. The class physical fitness activities will include an entry physical assessment as well as a continued evaluation of physical fitness activities throughout the course. Students are required to complete and record 30 minutes of some form of the following physical activity that include:

- Aerobic training and strength training
- Flexibility

- Sports and recreational activity

PURPOSE OF COURSE

The purpose of this course is to introduce students to the theories, purposes, and methods of Lifetime Wellness. The following are some of the benefits students will receive from the successful completion of this course. This course as offered will give students a foundation for developing procedures that will enable them to introduce lifetime wellness activities into their daily lifestyle. The course will give students the basic ideas, concepts, and knowledge for establishing a lifetime wellness program. The ability to succeed in this course will depend on a student's desire to succeed, the effort expended, and his or her depth of content understanding.

Students will gain a minimum level of knowledge of the principles of fitness, nutrition, weight management, behavior modification, and psychological well-being that can be used to improve their quality of life. It should be kept in mind, however, that the knowledge gained in this course is only the tip of the iceberg in a field of study that is ever changing.

To be completely successful, continued research and study will be necessary to gain the additional knowledge and fitness that go well beyond this course. When it is completed, students will have a background that will enable them to prepare personal fitness plans that can be used throughout their life. The introduction to this ISCL program begins with students outlining expectations that create students who are thoroughly informed of course requirements and organizational procedures, etc.

To assist the learning process this student handbook has been developed that contains a syllabus, course content, class organization, grading procedures, and other class assignments. A workbook is included that will provide the student with examples of projects to be observed and the objective of these features in order to create an effective and efficient learning environment in which students know in advance where the class is heading, what is required of them to meet individual group/team and class standards that have been established, and when work is due. This information will be discussed in great detail

An attempt to make course content more meaningful, up-to-date, and relevant to the students' needs is achieved by developing an instructional outline of student and class activities that can be revised in order to stay relevant to the students' efforts by keeping the content as up-to-date as possible. Good teaching is about humor and enjoying the learning experience. This can be accomplished through self-deprecating humor and the instructor not taking him- or herself too seriously, while maintaining a flexible but fixed agenda. This course of action will make their presentations more acceptable and help develop credibility.

CLASS RESPONSIBILITIES GUIDELINE

The following is a list of the procedures and class responsibilities that students must follow in order for the class to function at the highest level. Students must read it carefully and place a checkmark in the space provided at the end of each sentence and place their signature in the proper place.

- I will bring writing material and paper to each class session and record all pertinent and important information. ( )
- I will come to class prepared for all discussion questions to be completed on the day assigned. I understand that I will receive a failing/lower grade if I constantly come to class unprepared. ( )
- If I am absent from class on a group preparation or presentation day, I will type up the assigned questions to be turned in on the NEXT class meeting. ( )
- I understand that if my group cannot find the answer to the discussion question in the text, they must do an Internet or library search. All questions must be answered in full to be counted as complete, and one short sentence will not be enough information to answer most questions. ( )
- I understand that the text and research will not say, "This is the answer to question #1", etc., and that you may need to do some critical thinking, research, and reasoning when answering the questions. However, answers must be based on facts and conclusions derived from your readings and research. ( )
- If I come to class late, it is my responsibility to inform the instructor, or I will be credited with an absence. ( )
- I understand the following class procedures and the results that will occur for failure to live up to this contract agreement. ( )
- Signature_____ Date_____

CURRICULUM OBJECTIVES

The following is a list of the objectives that students will be accountable for knowing and understanding. These objectives include what this course is trying to achieve, how it will be achieved and under what conditions they will be completed. In addition to the specific Lifetime Wellness objectives listed below, several overall concepts such as improving problem-solving ability, communication skills, the ability to translate knowledge from one context to another, and other learning factors, could also be considered.

These objectives would also include the ability to make sound decisions through analytical reasoning, critical thinking, and problem solving. The teaching procedures will not be limited to the following key objectives:

- To learn and understand the foundation of physical development and general fitness strategies.
- To develop an understanding of the major factors of how to improve your life by making sound decisions in relation to stress, nutrition, weight control, and cardiovascular health.
- To develop the vocabulary, skills, methodology, and research tools basic to the course of study.
- To develop the knowledge and ability to research, write, and talk intelligently about physical fitness and health.
- To design a framework of factors that outlines a sensible physical fitness, behavior modification, weight management, nutrition, flexibility, and stress-management program.
- To understand the process of behavior modification in establishing an effective wellness lifestyle and to become knowledgeable about behavior mortification, sexually transmitted diseases, and addictive behaviors.

Each unit being studied will also have objectives and concepts specific to the material being studied. Because they are mandatory in developing new skills, goals will be established to help generate new ideas and evaluate existing behavior. Students must acquire the skills and work habits needed to also succeed in other courses and to achieve better opportunities in life. The ultimate goal is literacy as it specifically relates to this course and how these values are shaped and how our choices in life are determined. The following are the specific learning objectives to be achieved from the study of each course unit.

- To encourage regular study habits, have fun, and enjoy the learning process
- To review material covered in the text
- To prepare students for daily class activities
- To valuate instruction and student efforts
- To reinforce learning through additional repetition of material
- To involve as many of the senses as possible in each learning situation

HOW TO STUDY FOR THIS COURSE

Methods used in studying for this course are designed to provide students with information necessary for their success. Efficient study for this course begins with a thorough reading of the assigned text chapters. Information provided in the text will furnish students with a background knowledge and information about lifetime wellness that will be enhanced through videos, things to know and group discussion/lecture question and media presentations. When students begin to read the required text they will encounter many unfamiliar terms and details about wellness and fitness.

However, with diligent study, the knowledge necessary to make educated decisions regarding wellness/fitness, the concepts become clear. A review of the learning tools section of this handbook will provide students with the study skills necessary to succeed in this and other educational courses.

SELF-MANAGEMENT

After reviewing the course syllabus, handbook, text, and other responsibilities, students should consider what they want to accomplish in this course and plot what it will take to achieve their goals. They should ask themselves the following questions:

- What must be done to complete the course successfully?
- How much effort am I willing to put into the course?
- How can I put the time available to its best use?

The biggest key to efficient learning is the consideration of how to manage time wisely. Develop a weekly time schedule that organize available time by marking key dates, time in class, work time, free time, and study time. Study time should include time for reading, making useful notes, working on projects, and reviewing material to be prepared for evaluations.

Students must be flexible so that they can renegotiate their schedule, if necessary. The next order of business is to determine where and when you will study. Studying efficiency is increased if the student finds an area that is free from distractions. Learning is improved if students review course assignments periodically. Students should reward themselves when they achieve their goals.

STUDENT RESPONSIBILITIES CONTRACT

CONTRACT DEVELOPMENT: To be a successful secondary and college student, students must accept responsibility for what and how they learn. Learning requires students to make a commitment to get the job done, assume responsibility for their behavior, and realize that they will be held accountable for completing the contract. A student's first class project will be to develop his or her own contract.

122 *Appendix A*

This contract should be an outline of what the student wants to achieve from this class and how he or she intends to achieve success. The following is a sample outline of student responsibilities and a sample of a contract provided to give students a starting point. However, the contract belongs to the student and must be directed at what they want to achieve from this class. The student contract must be completed and signed on or before the second week of class.

This is a contract that states that, as member of the class, the student has reviewed and understands the learning requirements and class responsibilities. By signing this contract, students agree to adhere to the requirements for achieving the grade for which he or she has contracted. Agreeing to a grade to be achieved does not necessarily guarantee that the grade you have contracted for will be awarded unless all assignments are completed at the level required by the instructor. Check each entry located below to confirm that you have read and understand each item. Copy the entire contract and DATE AND SIGN.

THE CONTRACT: Contracts will be due one week after the first day of class.

SAMPLE OF STUDENT CONTRACT

STUDENT'S NAME _____
GRADE CONTRACTED FOR_____
CLASS
( ) **SYLLABUS:** I have read and understand the syllabus and workbook.

( ) **PANELS:** A list of panel discussions can be found in the workbook section. Review them and chose one that fits the student's interest. The student should not get involved in this assignment unless they intend to extend the effort required. All "A" students should be on a panel. However, being on a panel does not guarantee you an "A." Panel participants will be excused from an assignment of their choice and will be given class time for preparation. A list and date of panels will be posted in the classroom. The student will research and participate actively in presenting a panel.

( ) **TEXTBOOK:** Chapter highlighting or review assignments must be completed in a timely fashion.
( ) and will be collected and graded periodically.

( ) **LABORATORY ASSIGNMENTS**: Labs are located at the end of each text chapter. The instructor will inform students of assignments that must be completed on the second day of each unit. Lab assignments will be collected and evaluated and recorded.

( ) ORAL REPORTS: One 5-minute oral report is required on a topic pertaining to the units being studied or a related field. A list of these oral reports can be found in the workbook section. Topics must be relevant to the information being studied. The workbook contains information regarding the oral report and the proper format to be used in preparing reports. Oral reports must follow the oral report structure contained in the workbook. Although notes may be used, do not read the report. Be prepared to answer questions about the subject chosen.

( ) GROUP DISCUSSIONS/LECTURE PROJECTS: Participation and contribution to study a group is required of all students. Be prepared to assume leadership of group and class discussions. Groups will meet on days they are assigned to work on discuss questions to plan methods of research and how questions will be presented to class. Once group organization is complete, students can first work independently and then as a group to complete the assigned questions and prepare them for presentations. However, all discussion questions must first be answered individually, and students will be expected to participate in class discussions by asking questions and critiquing student presentations.

( ) PROJECTS: Five or six individual/group projects may be required. The objective of these projects is to provide knowledge guidelines for efficient and effective study and presentations while instilling the desire to continue with these programs after completion of this course.

( ) ATTENDANCE: Classroom and group attendance is mandatory and unexcused absences are not acceptable. However, personal, family, and school activities will be excused but a written note must be provided and all assignments must be completed.

( ) PARTICIPATION: Student participation in classroom and group projects will constitute a major portion of their class grade. This will be determined by the instructors and group members.

( ) GROUP DISCUSSION/LECTURE/THINGS TO KNOW PROJECTS: A list of discussion/lecture questions and things to know for each unit studied can be found in the workbook. The textbook, instructor, other research, and group discussions will provide the answers to these questions. Each question will be discussed by the class as a whole, followed by a PowerPoint presentation.

( ) INDIVIDUAL PROJECTS: May be assigned and presented orally in order to make up for missed assignments, to improve a grade, or as assigned by the instructor.

( ) VIDEO /POWERPOINT REVIEWS: Questions to be answered during a video or PowerPoint presentation can be found in the workbook and will be discussed as a group and/or the entire class.

( ) EVALUATIONS: Besides the pre- and post-knowledge reviews, no midterm or final will be required of students who have completed all class projects. You will be evaluated on attendance and class participation, quality of projects, completion of lab assignments, and chapter and video review in addition to things to know and an outline of each chapter/unit studied. I have read and understand the syllabus, class assignments, work deadlines, and the requirements of this contract. I realize that all requirements listed above must be performed at a high level of competency. I understand that class work is due on the date assigned. If I am absent on the day class work is due and it is not turned in prior to the absence, then I will receive no credit for this assignment.

Name:_____Date_____

LEARNING CONTRACT

A learning contract provides a vehicle for planning the learning experience and setting achievement goals which is a mutual undertaking between the instructor and student. Students participate in the process of diagnosing personal needs as a means of determining objectives to be achieved, identifying resources and choosing strategies, and evaluating accomplishments. By completing this process, it is hoped the student will develop a sense of ownership and commitment to the learning process. The student motivation requires their imaginative, creative, and analytical skills in completing contract requirements.

The following is a list of information required to complete the learning contract:

- Diagnose the components for successful performance in this course and determine how they will be achieved.
- Determine your learning objectives (what you want to learn) and establish goals.
- Specify the learning resources and strategies (how you will learn).
- Determine how you will show what you have learned.

- Set realistic target dates for completion of required course assignments.
- Complete the contract checklist to determine if you fulfilled the contract and with what level of success you want to achieve.

LEARNING STYLE INVENTORY

While a formal self-evaluation is beyond the scope of this syllabus, included is an informal learning style inventory (developed by Neil Fleming and Richard Fielder) to help students identify how they learn. This learning style assessment will help students find out about their preferred learning method. Research done on the left versus right brain found differences in relation to personality and has shown that people have a preferred learning style. The answers students give to the 14 questions found in appendix D will provide an indication of what their learning style tends to be. The learning style that has the highest score a student receives may describe what learning style is most appropriate for that student.

Remember, there are no wrong answers and none of the learning styles appear to be better than the others. Students may find that two styles receive approximately equal scores. This means that a student may prefer to use a combination of those two learning methods. An analysis, assessment, and self-evaluation of learning styles can be found in the learning section of appendix D.

STUDY SKILLS

NOTE TAKING: Success in class requires that students keep current with all assignments prior to class and group lectures/discussions. All assigned study discussion questions, video questions, and other assignments must be completed in a timely fashion. The student's study group is the place to discuss class activities (take notes). In addition, making useful notes from readings and lectures is an important study skill that can help students learn, recall, and review information.

Useful study notes are those that are correct and accurate. Student notes should be written in their own words and reflect what they think is important about information from readings, lectures, labs, discussions, etc.

The following is a list of efficient note-taking procedures that will help improve listening, retention, and recalling skills:

- **IMPORTANCE OF EFFICIENT NOTE TAKING**: Student-centered-learning instructors' lectures are short and only emphasize ideas of major importance. Therefore, taking good notes may enable you to answer exam and study questions without a great deal of research. Making good notes

reinforces main points through repetition and promotes active listening and improves concentration focus.
- **KEYS FOR IMPROVING NOTE TAKING**: Notes are easier to recall if students regroup material under key headings and put notes into an outline or mind-mapping format. It is also important for students to keep up with the speaker when taking notes by paraphrasing and synthesizing main ideas and then putting them into the student's own words. Date all notes, write legibility, don't erase or worry about spelling and punctuation when taking notes. This can be corrected when the notes are rewritten.
- **PRIOR TO CLASS OR GROUP WORK**: Complete or review assigned readings, vocabulary words, and discussion questions by making a brief organized set of notes. Briefly review notes from previous class activities prior to the beginning of the next group or class meeting. The student should include any questions or ideas they do not understand about how to complete the assignments and discuss them with their teammates or instructor.
- **DURING CLASS/GROUPWORK**: Summarize your instructor's and group's insights by searching for the main points, concepts, and themes put forth by the speaker and study group.
- **AFTER GROUP WORK**: Review and expand notes as soon as possible. Rewrite notes to include the new insights and questions proposed in class and groups. Periodically review and rewrite notes to clarify issues as new information becomes available.
- **SELECTING A NOTE-TAKING STYLE:** After reading the text and listening to lectures and group discussions summarize what you have learned by paraphrasing the information into your own words. The act of writing this information down helps students remember, recall, reinforce, and review information for evaluations and discussions. Notes can be organized into a graphic of the information by putting them into outlines, flowcharts, trees, or a mind-concept map. Mind-concept maps are thought to be most helpful in that material is organized in the way we think.

Mind mapping begins by placing a central idea in the middle of a piece of paper and adding related ideas by drawing lines to them from the central idea. Each sub-idea can be further divided. These lines represent a relationship between each of the ideas so new concepts can be added to them by drawing additional lines.

COMMUNICATION: THE KEY TO LEARNING

Communication is a two-way street that consist of both effective speaking and efficient listening skills in the classroom and small groups. Regular and open oral communication in which students share their thoughts and ideas in the classroom and small groups are a must for success. When students communicate openly in class activities, they develop a healthy learning environment by incorporating the following three components of feedback: instructor comments, reflective class, and group discussions, Peer group assessment and self-reflection will greatly improve student communication skills. To perform with success, students need to encompass the following effective oral communicators.

- Display the ability to explain your own ideas and thoughts clearly.
- Display the ability to express how you feel in an open and non-threatening manner.
- Ask questions that will help other students put forth their ideas and emotions.
- Sense how other students feel based on their nonverbal communication.
- Initiate conversations that relieve tension that seem to be brewing.
- Discuss the activities and interactions and encourage others to do the same.

Although a majority of the time in the class will be spent in developing speaking skills, students will also need to improve their ability to listen effectively. Research indicates that about 53 percent of time spent in class is consumed with the listening process, 17 percent reading, and 14 percent waiting for something to happen. Furthermore, less than 50 percent of the entire communication process will be remembered. Listening plays an even greater role in learning when we consider the time spent in group work, where the majority of studying time is spent gathering information and knowledge. The following steps can improve student listening ability.

- Take listening seriously: Make a self-listening inventory by analyzing your shortcomings.
- Prepare to listen: Learn all you can about the subject-situation before you attend the class or study group.
- Minimize physical barriers to listening by sitting in a position where you can observe and hear the presenter free from internal and external distractions.
- Have a specific purpose for listening: Analyze the message to focus listening by identifying the central theme and main points that are being presented. Think along with the presentation in group/class discussion by listening for evidence that supports the main points being made.
- Make use of the time difference between speaking and listening ability: This can be achieved by actively thinking about what is said and by taking efficient notes that summarize and review what has been said.

- Focus on the matter rather than the manner: Don't be distracted by location in which the listening takes place and by the speakers' delivery and appearance: which requires putting aside preconceived judgments
- Be an active listener: Active listening requires you to think a little ahead of the person who is making the presentation and try to anticipate what will come next.
- Practice—Practice—Practice: Your oral and listening skills whenever possible.

READING TO LEARN

Reading to learn is a specialized form of reading that requires effort. The following steps will improve your understanding of the material you read. The text plays an important role in almost all educational classes in that it is a student's Bible, the place to turn to when information and data are needed. The following are ways to get the most out of the text and other sources that you read from a book or Internet.

When reading a chapter in the text or other student reading sources of information, concentrate on the main ideas rather than details. Highlight these ideas with a marker as you read each section. After attending class or completing further study, reread the chapter and highlight any new ideas that appear.

The following are skills that will improve student reading ability.

- **READ WITH A PURPOSE**: The student should determine if they are reading to get a general idea of the material or for close scrutiny to detail. They should adjust reading speed and process accordingly. Read for main ideas by turning titles and headings into questions. In your first reading of a chapter in the text, concentrate on the main ideas rather than the details. After attending class or completing further study, reread the chapter and highlight any new ideas
- **PREVIEW THE TEXT**: Examine the table of contents to get an idea of how the book is structured and topic content. Briefly inspect the book chapter by chapter. Survey the index which is the key to locating data quickly. Check all titles, charts, graphs, maps, photos, summaries, and introductions.
- **REVIEW EACH CHAPTER, INCLUDING GRAPHS-CHARTS-PICTURES**: Quickly thumb through each chapter briefly and observe the major headings.
- **EXAMINE SUPPLEMENTAL DATA**: Review text timelines and outlines provided by the author. Inspect the supplemental reading material.

Read chapter summaries and answer any study questions included at the end of each chapter.
- **QUESTION THE TEXT**: Since headings generally reflect the main ideas of the text, formulate questions about the content by changing each heading or title into a question. When completing a section or a chapter in the text, see if you can answer the questions you developed.
- **REREAD EACH CHAPTER TO CHECK FOR UNDERSTANDING**: As you reread a chapter, highlight any new ideas or concepts with a different color marker. Make notes in margins and outline key phrases. Upon completion of each chapter, summarize the main ideas and concepts by writing them in your own words. Other useful recall techniques include visualizing the information as you read it, relating key concepts and ideas to something you already know, read out loud, and discuss the reading with someone else
- **REVIEW:** Examine information in the text by rereading your notes, questions, or exercises that have been developed from previous readings. Additional review techniques are to use index cards to review key terms and recite information out loud or explain the information to someone else (if you can do this, learning has taken place).
- **UNDERLINING/HIGHLIGHTING THE TEXT**: When highlighting information in the text, it is not the actual highlighting that helps you learn but the process of deciding which information is important enough to highlight. As you read the text, avoid the common pitfall of highlighting everything you read by highlighting only the main ideas. Be selective by highlighting only short segments of relevant information.
- **STUDYING WITH OTHERS:** One of the best ways to study and learn is by studying with someone else. Your understanding of the material is clarified when you must present ideas so that others can understand them. Organize a study group. Get to know students in your class/group and suggest that you work together. As a group, review and answer any questions you have and discuss what you believe are the major points. Formulate or use available test items to quiz each other; besides it's a good way to get to know others in the class.

Appendix B

Department of Physical Education and Health

HOW TO USE THIS SYLLABUS

This student syllabus, learning tools, and workbook are designed to guide students through the course of learning they have chosen. They will be provided with an outline of the basic structure that begins with a course overview. This overview describes the general scope of the course and what each main section being studied is about. Tools for independent learning are a condensed review of suggestions on how to study. These "tools" for learning contain a variety of study skills and helpful hints for independent, efficient study.

The workbook that accompanies the syllabus also explains exactly what is expected of each student, what is required for him or her to complete each unit, and the concepts the instructor considers important.

Each student must carefully review the information contained in the syllabus and workbook. The main text of this workbook is composed of 13 units. Each unit contains chapter and video reviews, things to know, reference lists, and group discussion/lecture questions and other important items. Each unit is a study guide and instructive tool that will help students in their study of Lifetime Wellness. Units I through IV provide an introduction to the course and the Principles of Wellness. Units V through X are designed to help students develop the knowledge and skills to change behavior and develop nutritional and fitness plans that can be used throughout a student's lifetime.

Units XI to XIII discuss the psychological factors of addictive behaviors and sexually transmitted diseases that hinder a wellness lifestyle. Unit checklists are provided that describes what is required in each unit and can be used to help students complete unit assignments. Each unit in the workbook contains the following items:

- Things to know: a list of vocabulary words or concepts that will guide students in their reading and are important to understanding wellness.
- Chapter reviews: questions that are designed to increase student understanding of the main concepts the instructor feels are important and provide both student and instructor feedback regarding chapter knowledge
- Reference lists: provide supplemental information that will add to student knowledge regarding the topic of each unit.
- Video reviews: a list of questions that provide additional information and may provide a different viewpoint regarding information being studied.
- Discussion/lecture questions: provide an interactive, problem-solving approach that requires creativity, critical thinking and analytical reasoning to complete this group project. Students will be given class time to assign and organize group presentations. Library and Internet research will be needed to answer some questions and provide information for other projects.

CLASS ORGANIZATION AND STRUCTURE

The curriculum to be taught in the Lifetime Wellness course is divided into two segments: The first segment consists of lifetime wellness studies and the second, physical fitness training. Only the in-class portion is presented in this study. Lifetime Wellness is divided into 13 units, which consist of the following topics:

WEEK 1—UNIT I Class introduction—consists of the Handbook, Syllabus, and Workbook
WEEK 1—UNIT II Introduction to Lifetime Wellness
WEEK 2—UNIT III Fitness assessment
WEEK 3—UNIT IV Developing a fitness plan
WEEK 4—UNIT V Behavior modification and wellness
WEEK 5—UNIT VI Body compositions and weight management
WEEK 6—UNIT VII Wellness diet
WEEK 7—UNIT VIII Aerobic fitness
WEEK 8—UNIT IX Muscular fitness
WEEK 8—UNIT X Flexibility
WEEK 9—UNIT XI Psychological well-being
WEEK 10—UNIT XII Addictive behaviors
WEEK 10—UNIT XIII STD and other diseases

Appendix B

TENTATIVE COURSE CALENDAR

This is a sample of a tentative course outline designed to give students an approximate timetable and the order in which the class activities will take place. It is a breakdown of the time that each unit will take to complete. However, due to unforeseen factors, it may differ from time to time in the time required to complete each unit. This, of course, will change to fit the curriculum being taught and the textbook being used. For the purpose of this book, it has been limited to the first 4 weeks of the course.

WEEK 1: UNIT I CLASS—INTRODUCTION TO UNDERSTANDING THE HANDBOOK, SYLLABUS, AND WORKBOOK
  Readings: Review Handbook, Syllabus and Workbook
  Lecture/Discussion and questions regarding the Syllabus

Pre-Wellness Reviews

UNIT II: INTRODUCTION TO WELLNESS

  Readings: Chapter 1 Physical Fitness, Health and Wellness, pp. 1–26
  Labs
  1.1 Identify Your Health Strength and Weaknesses, p. 15
  1.2 Assessing Your Health Risks, p. 17

WEEK 2: UNIT III—FITNESS ASSESSMENT

  Readings: Chapter 2 Assessing Your Present Levels of Fitness, pp. 21–49
  Labs:
  2.1 Your Physical Fitness Profile, p. 35
  2.3 Determining Your Resting and Exercise Heart Rate, p. 49
  Physical Evaluation
  Student Reports: Hydration—Hypothermia
  Project #1: A Physical Appraisal—Panel

WEEK 3: UNIT IV—DEVELOPING A FITNESS PLAN

  Readings: Chapter 4 Principles of Fitness, pp. 67–88
  Labs:
  4.1 Choosing and Committing to Exercise, p. 83
  4.2 Finding Your Target Heart Rate, p. 87
  Readings: Chapter 15 Designing a Program Unique to You, pp. 367–399
  Labs: 15.1 Why I Want to Be Physically Fit, p. 391
  15.2 Developing a New Mindset about Exercise, p. 393
  15.3 Which Sports Match Your Personality?, p. 395
  15.5 Guides to Developing a Program Unique for Each Student, p. 399
  Student Reports: Principles of Overload—Specificity—Recuperation

WEEK 4: UNIT V—BEHAVIOR MODIFICATION AND WELLNESS

Readings: Chapter 3 Behavioral Change and Motivation Techniques
Labs:
3.1 Locus of Control Assessment, p. 61
3.2 Alienation Assessment, p. 63
3.3 Body Self-Esteem Assessment, p. 65
Student Reports: Locus of Control—Removing a Bad Habit
Project #3 Changing for the Better

COURSE REQUIREMENTS

Like all educational courses, this course has specific requirements. Students are required to attend classroom presentations and participate in groups and other activities as part of their in-class responsibilities; in addition students will be required to present and participate in the following activities:

Chapter Reviews: In order to better understand the text and concepts considered important by the instructor, students will be asked to answer chapter review questions found in their workbook. These questions are used to increase understanding of material in the text. They will be researched and discussed in groups and presented to the class.

Things to Know: This is a list of vocabulary terms that, when understood, make learning course content much easier. Things to Know are found in the workbook and will be covered in text, videos, and discussions. Things to Know will be discussed in groups and class meetings.

Group Lecture/Discussions: Students must read each chapter in the text as required and answer the discussion/lecture questions prior to group activity. Only with prior preparation will this type of active learning be effective. The Internet, videos, and books on call in the library can be used to assist the students and groups in preparing for their assignments. Extra credit will be given to group leaders who lead the research and assignment discussions.

Videos Reviews: Periodically videos will be shown when possible for their educational value. Students must answer the video review questions in the workbook during the video. Videos are shown to provide different viewpoints on what is being studied and as repetitions of material previously studied and to make the class more enjoyable. Questions will be discussed first in groups and then in class.

Lab Assignments: Lab assignments are found at the end of each chapter in the text. They must be completed after you have read each chapter. These exercises are important in increasing self-knowledge and understanding of wellness concepts. They may be required as an oral report

Oral Reports: Oral reports will be assigned, presented, and discussed in the class, and the information must be relevant to the unit being studied. Check the tentative course outline in the Syllabus and activities section of each unit's introduction for the approximate time oral reports are due. Be sure to follow the proper procedures for presenting an oral report that are found in the learning skills section of the workbook.

Individual Projects: Several 1–2 page projects on the subject being studied may be assigned at the end of each unit. Check the individual projects assignment section found in most units of the Syllabus. Students must follow the project organization, format, and content as outlined.

Panel Discussions/Debates: Several panels will be presented as time permits during the quarter. Check the panel assignment sheet in the syllabus and choose a panel that interests you. In order to receive an "A" grade in this class you must actively participate in a panel. The facilitator will assign the topics and time for delivery of panel discussions.

Group/Individual Presentations: Each member of a group will be assigned a chapter discussion question by the group leader. These questions will be discussed as a group in preparation for each individual presentation of the assigned questions to be discussed by the class. Each student and group must spend time answering all questions presented by the class.

PowerPoint Presentation: The instructor will review the discussion questions and other pertinent information at the close of each unit with a PowerPoint presentation.

Progress Reviews: There will be a short progress review given periodically during the quarter. If you have perfect attendance, you will be excused from taking some of these exercises. They may be taken, however, for extra credit once this course requirement has been fulfilled. Students should have covered the assigned learning material in at least 5 or 6 repetitions: these repetitions consist of reading the text, group and individual discussions, class presentations and discussions, and video and PowerPoint presentations.

Appendix B

GOAL DEVELOPMENT

GOAL SETTING—THE MAGIC LIST: Attainable goals are the student's roadmap to success. Students must set both short-term and long-term goals and establish a time frame in which they should be achieved. Research indicates that learning is most effective if goals are established that solve the problems faced by the student. To be successful, goals must be realistic, attainable, and written down and a date set for completion. Most teachers know, and students must understand, that programming for success requires "motivational management" through goal setting. Setting goals is the key to motivation and a sign of good planning.

The objectives of goal setting are to maximize learning performance, to control and direct behavior in the right course of action, and to achieve optimal personal growth and development. Commitment is created when goals are established that are important to the student. Performance, motivation, and success have been shown to be directly related to a factor called the "goal set sequence": Goal setting leads to motivation; motivation leads to achievement, and achievement leads to success, and it's never ending. Based on intrinsic motivation, the drive to achieve must come from within the learner. That is, the goals that are set must be the student's choice; they must be what he or she wants to achieve in life and education. Developing goals is an act of preparedness by designing the body and mind to execute with effort correctly in order to become successful. More importantly, students must understand that there are no shortcuts to goal achievement. To be attainable, goals must be realistic and measurable in order for us to determine if they have been achieved.

Dr. Parham, a UCLA consulting psychologist, suggested that goal setting is a central component to success and improvement. His studies indicate that goals allow students to identify where they may be in the future, which stimulates thinking regarding the steps they will need to take and the required strategies and timetable needed to reach their goals. In addition, goal setting provides a means for evaluating performance and seeing the big picture. Dr. Parham outlines the following four factors that are crucial for goal achievement and success: 1) appropriate reinforcement, 2) support, 3) discarding the fear of success, and 4) removing the fear of failure.

Most psychologists believe that it is very challenging and may be nearly impossible to be successful and perform at extremely high levels if goals have not been established first. Goal development is a student's blueprint for success if they are achievable and not beyond a student's reasonable expectations. Therefore, goals must be specific, positive, and personal aims that are clearly defined and understood by the student. They are the student's wishes, desires, and dreams. In developing a goal-setting program, a student must consider the following factors:

- Set long-term, short-term, and specific goals—performance goals provide the best results.
- Evaluate goals on a regular basis to keep them pertinent and up-to-date.
- Set challenging but realistic goals.
- Individualize goals, and set only those goals to which you are willing to commit.

Goals that begin as dreams or aspirations can provide a student with a tremendous amount of desire, direction, and perspective. Furthermore, as students turn their dreams and aspirations into specific goals and plans, a clearer picture of what they are trying to achieve will emerge to direct their actions. To be successful, specific goals must be both appropriate and attainable. Thus, the goals chosen must be difficult enough to provide a challenge yet appropriate enough to allow for accomplishment. These factors will enable the student to realize concrete progress through consistent goal achievement.

Once this is accomplished, confidence will increase that in turn fuels the momentum for achieving higher aspirations. Achieving success requires that long-term goals, specific intermediate, and short-term goals must be established. Short-term goals are like the steps in a ladder in that each step brings the student closer to achieving his or her long-term expectations. Studies of successful students indicate that when establishing specific goals, they must be flexible enough to allow for adaptation and adjustment. Flexibility allows ambitions to adjust to the environmental conditions as the situation dictates.

The more specific the goal, the more control a student has over circumstances that arise in the environment and the less that is left to chance. Remember, a student charts his or her course, and only he or she knows what direction they are going in and can determine where the wind will take them. Students often ask the question, "What is the purpose of goals?" The answer is that goals are the plans that give a student control over behavior and the direction in which goals will take them and adds focus to life. For, without goals, it is difficult for achievement to take place. An effective goal-establishment program must be tied together with well-defined, measurable goals.

The goal-setting process can be used to incorporate the mental aspects of a learning process. Goals that are written down and reviewed periodically are reminders to the student of what he or she is trying to achieve. In addition, they encourage efficiency and provide a means for summarizing and evaluating performance achievement. Although some goals may not be reached, the key to success and achievement is for the student to give his or her best effort regardless of the results. Moreover, while pursuing the desired objective, the student will come to realize that the effort expended toward reaching the desired goals may even be more important than actual goal achievement.

A student's guide to successful goal setting should include the following factors:

- Review existing levels of development to decide the desired level to be achieved. Identify goals that are meaningful and achievable.
- Determine if goal achievement is worth the sacrifice that is required.
- Set realistic specific goals that can be accomplished in a reasonable time frame.
- Set new goals if old goals appear unrealistic or hinder motivation/improvement.
- Establish goals that can be evaluated. Institute positive goals.
- Set goals that are specific to the nature of the tasks being performed.
- Work with teachers and group/team members to establish team as well as individual goals.
- Put your goals in writing in order to make a commitment to achievement.

GOAL ESTABLISHMENT

The following is an outline format for setting success goals. Add others that you think are important.

WHAT ARE YOUR LIFETIME GOALS?
1. _____
2. _____
3. _____
4. _____

HOW WILL GOALS BE ACHIEVED?
1. _____
2. _____
3. _____
4. _____

LIST YOUR EDUCATIONAL GOALS.
1. _____
2. _____
3. _____
4. _____

HOW WILL GOALS BE ACHIEVED?
1. _____
2. _____
3. _____
4. _____

LIST YOUR GOALS FOR THIS CLASS.
1. _____
2. _____
3. _____

HOW WILL GOALS BE ACHIEVED?
1. _____
2. _____
3. _____

Establishing the proper attitudes toward learning will improve the probability of achieving both the external and internal contest and should include the following rational perspectives. Two goals that seem to be the most effective in creating motivation and improving learning acquisition are success (achievement and performance) goals. Success goals are determined by what the student wants to achieve as a result of his or her performance goal achievement.

THE P'S AND D'S—KEYS TO ACHIEVING GOAL SUCCESS

1. THE "P'S" ARE THE KEYS.

   a. Perspective
   b. Persistence
   c. Purpose Positive
   d. Performance
   e. Pride
   f. Perfection
   g. Mental Attitude

If a student has a POSITIVE MENTAL ATTITUDE they see things in the right PERSPECTIVE. If a student sees things in the right PERSPECTIVE they have a PURPOSE for their actions. If a student has a PURPOSE they will be PERSISTENT in their drive to achieve success. If a student is PERSISTENT they can achieve PERFECTION in learning that will create PRIDE in PERFORMANCE which in turn develops the ultimate goal—a POSITIVE MENTAL ATTITUDE and a greater chance of educational success.

2. THE "D'S"—A STRAIGHT LINE TO STUDENT SUCCESS

   - Devotion
   - Desire
   - Dedication
   - Discipline

DEVOTION to achievement creates in the student the DESIRE to learn. The DESIRE to learn requires DEDICATION to be the best and demands considerable DETERMINATION. DETERMINATION to learning produces the DISCIPLINE needed to achieve. Achievement increases the DEVOTION to learning and the DESIRE to succeed.

Appendix C: Student Workbook

Class Organization and Structure

STUDENT ACTIVITIES AND DAILY SCHEDULES

Students should develop a daily schedule in which he/she records their activities for each hour of the day in order to determine time available for study, leisure activities, etc. The enclosed assignment report forms have been developed by the Instructor to provide an outline of what is required in the study of each unit.

The following pages contain samples of unit assignments that allow students to structure a process for studying and preparing for each unit to be covered. It gives students a complete review of all the activities that will be researched and prepared while acquiring individual knowledge and the ability to present information to their group and the class. The process will increase the time available during the semester for the instructor to spend with students.

INTRODUCTION TO THE COURSE OF STUDY
DATE_____ CLASS TIME _____ ACTIVITY TIME _____

ANNOUNCEMENTS
    1. _____
    2. _____
    3. _____
    4. _____

CLASS OBJECTIVES (25 min.): Upon completion of this lesson students will:

1. Understand and use the Syllabus and Handbook effectively
2. Have a complete knowledge of administration procedures and class requirements
3. Learn to assume responsibility for learning

UNIT CONCEPTS (35 min.)

1. The purpose of the course
2. An appreciation of fitness concepts
3. The tools of learning
4. The role of the handbook as a learning tool

UNIT OUTLINES (60 min)

1. Review of the syllabus
2. Introduction/administrative procedures
3. Learning and study skills.
4. Readings: Chapter 1 Text "Physical Fitness Health and Wellness," pp. 1–20
5. Lab 1.1 Identifying Your Health Strength and Weaknesses, p. 15
6. Lab 1.2 Assessing Your Health Risk, p. 17
7. Things to Know #1
8. Lecture/Discussion Questions #1
9. Student Reports #1. Hydration-Hypothermia
10. Reference List #1. Preventing Thermal Injuries

DAILY CLASS/ GROUP ACTIVITES
UNIT I—DEVELOPING A FITNESS PLAN
DATE_____ **CLASS TIME** _____ **ACTIVITY TIME** _____
ANNOUNCEMENTS
1. _____
2. _____
3. _____
4. _____

OBJECTIVES

1. To Understand Fitness and Its Effects on a Positive Lifestyle.
2. To Develop a Fitness Plan That Will Achieve Lifetime Fitness and Wellness

CLASS ACTIVITY
QUIZ: Definition of "Things to Know" #4—5 min.

CHAPTER REVIEW: #14 Designing a Program Unique to You—15 min.
LECTURE: How to pick a wife—Genie in a bottle (fun)—10 min.
STUDENT ACTIVITIES
GROUP LECTURE/DISCUSSIONS: #5 Where Am I Going?—50 min
Group Preparation—20 min.
Group Presentation Research—15 min.
Group Presentation—20 min.
Power Presentation # Cartoons
Developing a Fitness Plan PP #1-14
ORAL REPORTS (30 min.): Overload _____
Specificity: What is it? _____
Recuperation: How is it achieved? _____
VIDEO REVIEW (20 min.): #5 Fitness and Wellness/#6 Exercise and Health

GROUP AND INDIVIDUAL ASSIGNMENTS

1. Readings: Chapter 3 "Behavior Modification/Motivational Techniques," pp 51–66.
2. Lab 3.1 Locus of Control and Assessment, p. 61
3. Alienation Assessment, p. 53
4. Body Self-Esteem Assessment, p. 65
5. Discussion Questions #5 "Making Changes"
6. Things to Know #4
7. Reference List #3 Change
8. Reference List #4 Readiness for Change
9. Individual Projects #3 Changing for the Better

LEARNING TOOLS

Students are the center of the learning process. While the instructor can provide them with the guidance and materials that are needed for success, it is the student's responsibility to set goals, plan their work, take notes in class and group discussions, and read the text. An important process in efficient learning is to schedule the time needed to complete all assignments. Developing good study skills and habits will not only save students time and energy, but can help them learn, remember, and recall what they learn more effectively while reducing the guesswork so prevalent in education. Efficient learning is achieved by the following procedures:

- DEVELOP A KNOWLEDGE AND UNDERSTANDING OF THE LEARNING PROCESS. Pay attention in study sessions. Read and study the assignments given.

- ORGANIZE AND MAKE STUDY TIME EFFICIENT. Reduce the non-learning situations that take place during study time and understand the objective-organizational format for effective study.
- EXECUTE A MULTITUDE OF PERFECT/CORRECT REPETITIONS. Take advantage of every opportunity to improve. Lost study time and experiences can never be reclaimed. Make every effort to maximize every learning moment. Use the group members as sources of information.

The following is a list of the class requirement upon which student grades will be determined.

Lecture Discussion Questions, Things to Know
Video Reviews, Individual Oral Reports
Panel Presentations, Student Evaluation
Written Presentations, Group Evaluations
Written Exams

When preparing to work on the projects listed in the Workbook, students must refer to the Course Requirements in the Syllabus for the due data of each subject/project. The following are examples of student requirements for each unit being studied.

UNIT I—CLASS DISCUSSION QUESTIONS

These questions are designed to accomplish two important tasks: First, to explain why they are important and second, what main point they are trying to achieve. These questions are designed to create critical thinking and problem-solving situations.

1. According to this handbook, syllabus, or workbook, what is the best way to begin your course of study?
2. Explain the aspects of the handbook that will make learning easier. Why?
3. Explain the purpose of this course and how this purpose is to be achieved.
4. List and explain the objectives of the course.
5. What is the purpose of student evaluation and how are students assessed and evaluated in this course?
6. What are the results of not being prepared for group and other projects? What is the penalty for being absent during group preparation and discussion periods?
7. According to the facilitator, how many unexcused absences are students allowed? How many tardies count as an absence? What is the grade deduction for each unexcused absence or excessive tardiness?
8. Discuss methods by which you will be graded in this class and why they are important to learning.

9. Briefly explain the instructor's role in the organization and activities that take place in this course.
10. When developing an oral report, how should it be organized? What is the most important aspect in preparing to present an oral report?
11. Explain the format to be used when presenting a written report.
12. As far as preparing for a panel discussion, how should it be organized and what is the most important aspect to consider in presenting a panel discussion?

UNIT II—WELLNESS DISCUSSION QUESTION

In the study of student learning, research found that if students are left to explore required avenues through analytical reasoning and critical thinking, increased learning occurs. Furthermore, learning is more efficient if students inject their own ideas. Answer the following questions and prepare to discuss them in your group in addition to the class.

1. Define the term "wellness" as it relates to living a healthy and fitness lifestyle.
2. Identify and explain the five dimensions of wellness.
3. What factors should you consider when adopting a philosophy of wellness?
4. What are the 5 major components of fitness that affect a wellness lifestyle?
5. What factors should you consider when developing a positive wellness lifestyle?
6. What 3 factors have the most effect on people living a wellness lifestyle? How are they determined?
7. What are the benefits of choosing to live a wellness lifestyle?
8. How does age influence the lifestyle we live?
9. Who is responsible for the lifestyle we live, and what personal choices can we make to promote a healthy lifestyle?
10. Outline a self-step plan that will enable you to establish a wellness lifestyle.
11. What are the 4 reasons people fail to maintain lifestyle wellness programs?

UNIT III—VIDEO REVIEW
VIDEO REVIEW 1—FIT OR FAT

Students answer the following questions and prepare them for discussing in their groups and the class.

1. What is the greatest health behavior you can adopt?
2. What happens to sugar when fat people eat it?

3. Name the best type of cholesterol.
4. Where do women tend to lose fat first when exercising?
5. Define Lipo-genesis.
6. What purpose does fat play in the body?
7. If you are fat and continually dieting, what happens to the fat you lost when you stop dieting and why?

UNIT IV—THINGS TO KNOW
Define the following terms:
HEALTH
SPIRITUAL HEALTH
WELLNESS
SELF-EFFICACY
PHYSICAL HEALTH
BEHAVIOR MODIFICATION
SOCIAL HEALTH
MENTAL HEALTH
EMOTIONAL HEALTH
RISK FACTORS

PANEL/DEBATE GUIDELINES

OBJECTIVES:

- Students are called upon to take a side on an issue and defend their opinion.
- To analyze important issues critically and develop astute insights in order to reach intelligent conclusions.
- To develop an in-depth understanding of health and wellness concepts.
- To generalize, make inference, comparison and understanding.
- To emphasize the contributions of Wellness to healthful living.

TIME LIMIT: Instructor will set a time limit for each debater to present their line of reasoning.

PREPARATION: Pick a topic/s that is of great interest to you. However, the student should not sign up for a panel unless they are going to complete the assignment—the penalty will be severe for those who do not complete this assignment. Students should use concepts and questions prepared by the instructor as their research guideline. Be able to critique the opposing point of view by understanding research concepts from both sides of argument. Begin research of the topic by reading about the topic in the text; check the school library and text bibliography for additional references. Read and study the articles left on reserve in the library by the instructor. An Internet search is an excellent research source.

PROCEDURES: Meet with other members of the panel, and plan a strategy for research and presentation. Remember, class members will be asking debaters questions so they should practice and rehearse their presentation by having someone ask them questions. Students should make a nametag that can be seen by audience, indicating who they are and what they represent. For creditability, cite primary sources whenever possible.

PRESENTATION: Panel will begin with a brief introduction of the topic by the instructor. Prior to opening the panel to questions from the audience, panel members will make a short presentation and brief summary of the topic. This summary should be based on the side of the argument the student represents. Following these brief presentations, panel members will answer questions put to them by the audience or other panel members. Students should be prepared to summarize their beliefs at the conclusion of the panel presentation.

EXAMPLE OF SELECTED PANEL DISCUSSIONS

- Aerobic versus anaerobic fitness
- Natural vitamins versus vitamin supplements
- Dieting versus exercise for weight loss
- Is substance abuse a physical or mental problem?
- Alcohol versus drugs/aids versus other sexually transmitted diseases

DEBATES: Classroom debates empower learning in that it allows students to become involved in researching, teaching, and recognizing different points of view. The following are the benefits of the debate process:

1. Reduces biases
2. Improves student analysis of research skills
3. Promotes logical and critical thinking
4. Improves communication abilities
5. Increases student motivation
6. Builds team work skills

The debate proposition should be a carefully worded one sentence that calls for a change or the institution of a new proposition. Debating a topic offers the opportunity to discuss the issues presented by presenting facts and the debater's beliefs. This allows the debater flexibility in developing arguments.

Use affirmative or negative terms in an attempt to refute the arguments of the other side.

INDIVIDUAL ORAL REPORT
Probably no skill acquired in college will have a more direct carryover value into other school work, business associations, and professional life than the ability to deliver a good clear oral report in an interesting manner. The following are the steps a student must follow when they are giving an oral presentation.

PREPARATION OF REPORT: You should choose a topic that is of interest to you. You must follow the proscribed methods and sources in researching your topic. Adapt the material to your audience. Begin with the known if you want the audience to understand the unknown. Give a background on the subject of the report. Do not confine the report to just what you have read. You should give your opinion and thoughts when making conclusions.

- Introduction: Open with an attention-getting device. Make sure the nature and importance of topic is clearly understood.
- Preview the main points.
- The body contains the main points of the report.
- Speak loudly—use appropriate vocabulary. Give the source/s of your material.
- Remember the KISS principle (keep it simple, stupid).
- The student may use notes, but they should not read from them.
- Customize the pitch to be given by showing how and what is being presented will help the audience understand the presentation.
- Give them something to remember with a one-line catch phrase.
- Rehearse-rehearse-rehearse.
- Students must remember that enthusiasm matters so they must show a passion for their subject.
- Be sure to conclude with a bang—this is what the audience will remember best.
- DO NOT READ YOUR PRESENTATION/DELIVERY.

ORAL REPORT SELECTION: Students should review the items below and write a few words about each one to help them choose the oral report they would like to present to the class. The following are samples of the topic to be presented, However, if the student has a topic he/she likes better, discuss it with the instructor:

HYPOTHERMIA/ HYDRATION _____
PRINCIPLE OF OVERLOAD _____

PRINCIPLE OF SPECIFICITY _____
PRINCIPLE OF RECUPERATION _____
LOCUS OF CONTROL _____
REMOVING A BAD HABIT _____
BASIL METABOLIC RATE _____
SET POINT THEORY _____
EATING DISORDERS _____
OBESITY/ANOREXIA- B _____
THE FOOD PYRAMID _____

WRITTEN PRESENTATIONS

DEVELOPING A RESEARCH PAPER: The objective of this project is to give students experience in the methods of research and the interpretation of data when developing a written project. It also gives the instructor the opportunity to determine the student's ability to read and analyze critical issues and to make generalizations, inferences, and comparisons of the various ideas and concepts being studied. The Internet offers a tremendous source of research data. The instructor will generally have additional research sources on call in the library.

The first rule for the student to follow in their research is to know exactly what they want to research by making an outline, and he or she should start his or her investigation early. An investigation generally begins with a question or a problem to solve. Thus, the second step is for the student to select a manageable question they want answered. Once the student has determined the thesis (topic) they want to write about, they can begin their research by examining the material available to them in the library, etc. Encyclopedias offer a good introduction to a topic and will give a good overall background on the subject. This will also be a good source of additional research material.

Furthermore, if the student is not an expert, his or her ideas should not be used as the main source of data. Health and wellness journals of the various associations will provide good reference sources. The writing phase of student papers should start with the student making an outline of the major points presented on the topic. This will provide a general framework that gives direction to the narrative. Writing a paper for a difficult class project should be kept very simple and must follow prescribed guidelines.

Organizationally, the paper should contain an introduction, i.e., tell them what you're going to tell them, a body of main points, i.e., tell them what you want them to know, and a conclusion, which ties data together by summarizing your introduction and main points, i.e., tell them what you told them.

Remember, it's the conclusion that will generally be remembered. The manuscript should begin with a clear statement of the argument the student is proposing so that the reader will be able to follow and assess their narrative. The body or narrative should be organized in a logical sequence that presents the evidence in a convincing manner. Remember, any facts the students present in his or her narrative must be relevant to the central argument. Since knowledge changes over time, the narrative must redirect and connect diverse facts into a cohesive story. Do not translate from one main point to another without connecting the relevance of how the topics relate.

There are two types of informational sources that the student should be aware of once they begin their research: primary and secondary. Primary sources are the best and most accurate source of data. Primary sources are those written at the actual time of the event by people, in newspapers accounts, and in government records, etc. Review the glossary and index of the text for additional sources of information, etc. Secondary sources are those written after the fact by someone who is interpreting primary sources. The student manuscript is a secondary source.

In order for a writer's evidence to assume validity, they must cite their source. One of two types of citations can be used in this project when quoting or paraphrasing the works of another author. It may be done by either a footnote of the source at the end of the page or by citing the source in the text immediately before or after using the quote (see Sample 1/Sample 2 below). The students should base their paper on at least 3 to 5 sources of material and remember to include them in a bibliography at the end of the paper. The following are samples of the proper way to cite an author's work in an endnote, footnote, and in the bibliography.

CITING THE AUTHOR WITH A FOOTNOTE
Sample 1: Stunk, B., and White, J. *Effective Writing*, New Haven, Conn., University Press, 1979).

CITING AN AUTHOR IN THE TEXT
Sample 2: Successful writing requires substance, style, clarity, and succinctness. (Stunk and White, 1979).

CITING DOCUMENTATION IN THE BIBLIOGRAPHY
Stunk, B. and White, J. O. *Effective Writing*, New Haven: University Press. (1979).

The paper should be single spaced with one-inch margins. Do NOT COPY the information presented in the paper directly from the source (unless you document the source). In other words, it must be put into the student's own words. Don't be afraid to use the ideas of another author, just put them in your own words. Remember, "The shadow knows." The length of a paper depends what it takes to tell the story.

WRITTEN REPORTS IN ABSTRACT FORM: The purpose of these written exercises is to develop a greater depth of understanding by dealing with wellness facts and concepts through critical thinking. Written reports are to be short analytical papers written in one of the following styles. Each paper is to be single spaced with normal size 12 fonts. Proper grammar, punctuation, and source notation must be followed. Be sure to cite the source information in the bibliography.

- Include bibliographical data about author as follows, title of article, publisher, date of publication, place of publication, volume, page numbers.
- State the purpose of the article. Why was the article written and what does it attempt to do?
- Determine the source of material, primary or secondary, and what the basis for the article was.
- Provide a summary of the essentials of the article. This summary should be clear and concise.
- Review the main points of the article and include at least one quotation.
- Be sure to state your findings and conclusions.
- State the general significance of the article. Why is the article important, and what is the significance of the article to Lifetime Wellness?

ASSESSMENT/EVALUATION: REQUIREMENTS

Analyzing progress is an integral part of the learning process. Learner reviews, in this course, are used to measure progress and are basically employed as a learning tool to provide feedback about improvement in subject matter, knowledge, and other learning skills. As a learning device, reviews are used to advise students of their areas of strength and weakness so that a determination can be made in regard to how and where to direct their future efforts.

All major projects are open-book take-home exercises. It is suggested that students use their study groups to aid in developing material to be used in completing student projects and taking exams. With this being the case, some in-depth and critical thinking, creativity, and imagination is expected when solving the problems proposed by these projects. Students should synthesize their answers and eliminate unneeded psychobabble. Watch for plagiarism— be sure your answers are written in your own words. Grammar and spelling must be as expected of an educational paper.

All projects that are to be turned in to the instructor must be typed on 8x11 paper with one-inch margins and in Arial and size 12 fonts. Projects are limited to 2 pages in length and singled spaced. A combination of paragraph and an outline bulleted form provide the best method for completing most projects. All work is due on the date assigned and will not be accepted after the class meeting: on date due. Flat tires, broken computers, and other excuses will not be accepted. Class work will also not be accepted when placed under the instructor's door, placed in his or her mailbox or pinned to the wall outside the office.

Project assignments are located in the student handbook or will be given to students by the instructor. If a student perceives that a problem may arise, complete projects ahead of time. Chapter reviews, lecture reviews, video reviews, and discussion/lecture questions are used not only to provide background information, but also to reinforce learning through repetition.

These learning materials will be collected periodically on a random basis. Only the shadow knows when these items will be asked for, so keep work current. This may seem like a lot of work, but come project time the data collected will provide much of the information needed to solve problems presented by the assigned projects, thereby greatly reducing research demands.

STUDYING FOR EXAMINATIONS

Knowledge reviews are designed to see how much of and how well students have learned the information presented. Determining the factors of evaluation that affect a student's grade has been left to the instructor. The following are steps that will improve student assessment and evaluation skills.

BEFORE THE EXAM: Review the objectives emphasized in the text.

- In an open-book test, the instructor is generally looking for how well the student can demonstrate their understanding of course concepts. This type of evaluation will generally focus on how well students supported their position.
- The study process for open-book tests should be similar to objective tests. In both cases, the student will need to incorporate the use of broad concepts as well as specific points.
- It is important that students outline the main points in their readings, discussions, and lectures. Write and answer practice questions you think will be asked.
- Get involved in a students study group.

REVIEWING FOR AN EXAM:

- Start preparation early. Research shows cramming for an exam to be an ineffective learning device learning.
- Guess at what possible questions will be asked and answer them.

- The student should compare the course outline with their reading assignments and discussions to see if a subject appears on both. If the subject appears on both, it is probably an important issue that students should study and remember.
- Review key terms from text, lectures, discussion questions, and video reviews.
- Go over the main concepts of the course with someone who has taken the course before.
- Practice—Practice—Practice—Visualize.

TAKING EXAMS: Regardless of the type of exam the student takes, the following procedures apply:

- Get a good night's sleep before the test.
- Have sufficient writing equipment.
- Relax by deep breathing, using the diaphragm.
- Read the test directions carefully.
- Put your name on each page of the exam.
- Follow directions closely. Be positive.
- Choose essay questions with which you are familiar, and answer them first.
- Eat a nutritious breakfast.
- Get some light exercise before the exam.

PRE-EXAM—REVIEW FOR REASSESSMENT: Students will be given a pre-assessment of current knowledge about wellness at the beginning of the quarter/semester and a re-assessment of knowledge gained at the end of the course. The objective of these re-assessments is not only to give students feedback and reinforcement of their efforts during the course, but also to give the instructor a knowledge of how well students understood material being studied when results are compared to the pre-test.

GRADING PROCESS

STUDENT EVALUATIONS: The grade students earn communicates information about them to parents, professors, school administrators. and prospective employers. This information is used to show students' recent performance and will predict students' future abilities and accomplishment. The following grading guidelines make efficient the process of evaluating the student's ability to function. Assessments of performance are based on material presented in class lectures and discussions, class projects, and information found in the textbook, etc. However, class and group participation plays a big role in a student's final evaluations.

It is the student's responsibility to be prepared to participate daily in group and lecture discussion sessions by asking questions and by critiquing the work of others. Occasionally, students will be asked to evaluate their performance and compare the evaluation with the results actually achieved. Perhaps this will give the student and professor a better idea of how projects and other assignments should be completed in order to improve future performance. How students are graded is the province of the individual instructor. However, the grade students receive will generally be based on his or her mastery of the knowledge attained, skills developed, and effort expended.

More important than the grade earned is the progress students make toward achieving their desired goals. Students will be provided with many opportunities to demonstrate what they have learned about wellness and fitness. It is their responsibility to demonstrate their level of achievement. Students doing average work can expect to earn an average grade. However, consideration will be given to the fact that students come to this class with different levels of proficiency, ability, and maturity. The following are factors to be considered in assessing student performance.

ATTENDANCE POLICY: It is important to understand and appreciate that the course requires intense study and in-class and group participation to improve knowledge and performance. Therefore, students are expected to attend class on a regular basis. Only two unexcused absences will be permitted without a deduction in their grade. However, after a total of four absences the student's grade will be greatly reduced unless there are extenuating circumstances. Class starts at the time designated. Therefore, being late to class without a certified excuse or coming to class unprepared will create a grade reduction.

ASSIGNMENTS AND MAKEUPS: All written materials, reports, or written assignments must be turned in on the date due. Any written material to be handed in must be typed. Group or individual assignments are also due on date assigned. Assignments will not be accepted after due date. No exceptions will be made to the above policy, so please don't ask. Missed student reviews can be made up with the approval of the instructor.

However, grades will be lowered on makeups—late work or an additional assignment may be required. If the student is not satisfied with their effort on class projects and wishes to redo an assignment to improve their grade, they may do so. Please be advised that redoing projects does not always ensure a better grade. The best policy is for students to do their best the first time around. Late assignments cannot be redone.

GRADING CRITERIA   **GRADING SCALE**
Reviews—Class projects—exams   40%—1.4

Class participation   30%—1.2
Oral reports and other assignments   20%—1.0
Attendance   10%—.4
                            Total—4.0

KEY POINTS TO REMEMBER

The introduction to the class begins with the instructor discussing with the students what is involved in an ISCL approach to learning and covers the students' and instructors' roles in this learning process. To assist the learning process, a student HANDBOOK was developed that contains a SYLLABUS that lays out the class organization and A WORKBOOK that contains information regarding student learning activities and a daily schedule of the projects and assignments for achieving success in the class and to structure class activities to fit his or her schedule.

The objective of these attributes is to create an effective and efficient learning environment in which students know in advance where the class is heading, what is required of them to meet group/team and class standards that have been established, and when work is due.

- This information should be discussed in great detail during the first week of class and reviewed periodically throughout the quarter. The objective is to make course content more meaningful, up to date, and relevant to the student.
- This is achieved by developing an instructional outline of student and class activities that can be revised to stay relevant to the student needs while keeping content as up-to-date as possible.
- By maintaining a fixed but flexible agenda, the instructor and students remain flexible and fluid in reacting to the daily changing of circumstances taking place in the classroom. The key to the success of ISCL is to encourage learners to ask questions, and formulate their own hypotheses through a process of inquiry in which each learner plays an important role in their own learning success.

Appendix D

Additional Information

THE LEARNING PROCESS

DIFFERENT LEARNING STYLES: In establishing an efficient student-learning program, instructors must understand and develop a learning curriculum that recognizes and addresses the various learning styles of each individual student. With this in mind, the instructor should support each student in developing some knowledge and understanding of their chosen learning style. However, ascertaining the preferred learning style or styles of a student will not be as effective if the learning environment in the classroom is not beneficial to a student learning style. There are three major learning styles: auditory, visual, and kinesthetic (tactile). Most students learn best by a mixture of these three with other learning styles.

However, the following outline contains additional learning styles adapted by Carol Moore Learning Styles (1992) which will give the student insights to additional learning styles and will aid in creating the best learning conditions:

- **Auditory (Hearing):** Learning research indicates that the visual style may be the most effective. However, often there are students who learn best by auditory means such as listening in lectures and class discussions. Learners with this learning style learn best by information that has been presented vocally rather than reading about it. Listening to music is a common study technique for these students.
- **Visual (Seeing):** Visual learners benefit from a variety of visual stimulation that might include such things as reading, watching a demonstration,

looking at graphics, and highlighting important data to be learned in a text book.
- **Tactile (Feel):** Kinesthetic students learn by doing an activity and in hands-on situations that include writing things down, which makes learning less difficult and is the easiest way for them to learn.
- **Formal/Informal**: A more informal situation may present a better learning process for this type of learner than the traditional setting.
- **Noise/Quiet**: Distracting sounds may hinder learning for many students. Therefore, noisy distractions should be reduced or limited.
- **Temperature:** Students should come to class appropriately dressed in order to reduce the effect of room temperature's role in student learning.
- **Lighting:** A light level that is satisfactory to all students must be established.
- **Kinesthetic**: Constant movement by some students is not acceptable behavior.
- **Mobility**: Class procedures need to be constructed into 30 minute segments in order to reduce restlessness if students are required to be in a stable situation for long periods.
- **Lesson Structure**: Lesson structure will create a logical sequence of a lesson that provides the best objective and systematic steps needed to complete assignments.
- **Sociological**: Some students benefit from participating in group assignments and activities, while others may have difficulty in group participation. Therefore, self-learners need some leeway when dealing with group assignments.

LEARNING STYLES SELF-EVALUATION: The following is a composition of learning styles as developed by Richard Felder/Neil Fleming. V=visual, A=aural, R=read/write, K=kinesthetic

Directions: Choose the answer that best explains your preference in each situation and put the letter in the box.
1. You are about to give directions to a person. She is staying in a hotel in town and wants to visit your house. She has a rental car. Would you:
    V) draw a map on paper?
    A) tell her the directions?
    R) Write down the directions (without a map)?
    K) pick her up from her hotel in your car?
2. You are staying in a hotel and have a rental car. You would like to visit a friend whose address you do not know. What would you like him to do?
    V) draw you a map on paper.
    A) tell you the directions by phone.
    R) write down the directions (without a map).

Appendix D 159

    K) pick you up from your hotel in his car.

3. You have received a copy of your itinerary for a world trip that is of interest to a friend. Would you:

    V) show her on a map of the world?
    A) call her immediately and tell her about it?
    R) send her a copy of the printed itinerary?

4. You are going to cook a dessert as a special treat for your family. Do you:

    V) thumb through the cookbook looking for ideas from the pictures.
    A) ask others for advice.
    R) refer to a specific cookbook where there is a recipe you know about.
    K) cook something familiar without the need for instructions.

5. A group of tourists has been assigned to you to learn about national parks. Would you:

    V) show them slides and photographs.
    A) give them a talk on national parks.
    R) give them books on national parks.
    K) drive them to a national park.

6. You are about to purchase a new stereo. Other than price, what would most influence your decision?

    V) it looks really classy.
    A) a friend talking about it.
    R) reading details about it.
    K) listening to it.

7. Recall a time in your life when you learned how to do something like playing a new board game. (Try to avoid using a very physical skill like riding a bike.) How did you learn best?

    V) by using visual clues like pictures or diagrams.
    A) by listening to somebody explain it.
    R) by reading written instructions.
    K) by doing it.

8. Which of these games do you prefer?

    V) Pictionary
    A) Scrabble
    R) charades
    K) by doing it

9. You are about to learn to use a new program on a computer. Would you:

    A) call a friend and ask questions about it?
    R) read the manual that comes with the program?
    K) ask a friend to show you how to use it?

10. You are not sure whether a word should be spelled *dependent* or *dependant*. Would you:

    V) see the word in your mind and choose the way it looks best?
    A) sound it out in your mind?

R) look it up in the dictionary?
K) write both versions down?
11. Apart from price, what would most influence your decision on what textbook to buy?
V) it looks OK.
A) a friend talking about it.
R) you read a review about it.
12. A new movie has arrived in town. What would most influence your decision to go or not to go?
V) you saw a preview of it.
A) friends talk about it.
R) you read a review about it.
13. What is your guess about how you learn best?
V) visual cues
A) listening and discussing
R) reading
K) doing (i.e., touch, taste, smell, and feel)
14. Do you prefer a professor who likes to use:
V) flow diagrams, charts, slides?
A) discussions, guest speakers?
R) handouts, textbooks?
K) field trips, labs, and practical sessions?

Totals: V____ A____ R____ K____

JUST A FEW EXAMPLES OF PROPOSED LEARNING THEORIES

Behaviorism	Informal and post-modern theories,
Conditioning	Multiple intelligences
Cognitive	Philosophical anthropology,
Constructivism	Instructional theory
Transformative learning theory	Criticism of learning theory,
Educational neuroscience	Learning by teaching
Brain-based theory of learning	Educational psychology,
	Instructional design
	Andragogical learning theory
	Learning style theory
	Cultural-historical psychology

COLLABORATIVE LEARNING
ADDITIONAL BENEFITS AND STRATEGIES OF COLLABORATIVE LEARNING

- Promotes and advances interpersonal relationships
- Institutes high expectations for students and teachers
- Advances higher accomplishment and class attendance.
- Students remain on task more and are less disorderly
- Produces a stronger social support structure
- Students develop more positive attitude toward teachers, principals, and other school personnel
- Establishes a more positive attitude by teachers toward their students
- Focus on learning style disparity among students
- Encourages modernism in teaching and classroom techniques
- Classroom is similar to real life, social, and job situations
- Anxiety in the classroom is significantly reduced
- Students discover alternate problems resulting in a safer environment
- Students perform modeling, social, and work-related tasks
- Endorses student-faculty interaction and familiarity
- Establishes an environment that is actively involved in exploratory learning
- Develops student self-esteem
- Increases positive race relations
- Creates positive heterogeneous relationships

STRATEGIES FOR EFFECTIVE COLLABORATION

- Minimal Instructor participation in class and group discussions
- Build up study group interdependence
- Sustain small groups
- Institute peer evaluations
- Group project evaluations
- Reinforce peer instruction
- Make available understandable instructions, assignment overviews
- Maintain heterogeneous groups
- Make the important work visible
- Assign student control
- Set up meaningful mini due dates
- Make the learning personally appropriate
- Support questioning
- Provide students with feedback regarding their discussion
- Impart timely and thorough group and individual feedback

CONSTRUCTIVE LEARNING

The following are several strategies; activities and methods used by constructivist educators in developing a CONS student-centered learning process. A constructivist approaches can also be used in online learning. For example, tools such as discussion forums, wikis, and blogs can enable learners to actively construct knowledge. A contrast between the traditional classroom and the constructivist classroom is illustrated below:

CONSTRUCTIVIST TEACHING STRATEGIES

- Promote and accept student autonomy and initiative.
- Attempt to use raw data and primary sources in addition to manipulative, interactive, and physical activities.
- Assign tasks to the students by using cognitive terminology such as "classify," "analyze," "predict," and "create."
- Use student responses when making instant decisions about teacher behaviors, instructional strategies, activities, and content being taught
- Explore students' understanding and prior experiences about a concept before teaching it.
- Encourage communication between the teacher and students and between the students.
- Support student critical thinking and inquiry by asking them open-ended questions and encourage them to ask questions to each other.
- Seek elaboration and ask follow-up questions after a student's initial response.
- Make sure to wait long enough after posing a question so that the students have time to think about their answers and be able to respond thoughtfully.
- Make available enough time for students to construct new learning on their own

EXAMPLES OF CONSTRUCTIVIST ACTIVITIES

In the constructivist classroom, students work primarily in groups where learning and knowledge are interactive and dynamic. There is a great focus and emphasis on social and communication skills as well as collaboration and exchange of ideas.

- **Experimentation**: Students individually perform an experiment followed by discussing the results as a class.
- **Research projects**: After researching a topic, students can present their findings to the class.
- **Field trips**. As a result of these trips students develop concepts and ideas that resemble the real world and can be discussed in class.
- **Films/videos**. Provide visual context in additional learning skills.

- **Class discussions.** This technique is one of the most important characteristics of constructivist teaching methods.

ESTABLISHING A GROUP/TEAM ENVIRONMENT

According to CTE Teaching Tips teamwork is an important characteristic of student centered learning in that teamwork skills become essential in a complex learning environment that demands multiple skills. In addition, studies indicate that students learn best from assignments that involve doing tasks as a team or when engaged in social interactions. Teamwork functions best in small groups that require students to attend to the atmosphere within their team, to build strong communication skills while integrating three basic feedback skills that include written or oral comments by the instructor, perceptive group discussions, and self-expression.

The following effective, intellectual, and emotional communicators could be included:

- The competence to express their beliefs in an open non-threatening method
- The ability for every member to voice his or her own ideas
- An important factor in effective communication is the capability to pay close attention to others
- Asking questions that improve understanding about teammates ideas and emotions
- The proficiency to interpret the nonverbal communication of how others feel
- The capability during tense circumstances to initiate dialogue with others
- Interacting and persuading others on the team to interact with their teammates
- An enhancement of team atmosphere will take place when communication is open

According to the NDT Research Center, there are differences in how students contribute as individuals or as a group or team. Since this document is based on students working as a team to produce a product, the following are some suggestions that are effective in a team's improvement proposed by Larson and LaFaston 1989: Each individual and team member must have clearly defined goals. Team goals should require specific performance goals/objectives that are laid out in concise terms so that the entire team knows when the goals/objectives have been achieved. The following are some of these goals.

1. Each team member must have a results-driven attitude. The team operates with an approach that generates the best results. It usually is of

utmost importance for a team to develop an operational structure with effective leadership.
2. All team members must be capable and well-informed in regard to the problem/assignment to be achieved.
3. A united dedication of all team members is a most important factor in directing and achieving team goals. Individual efforts to achieve personal goals are not allowed at this point.
4. A collaborative learning environment must be established that produces trust, honesty, and openness in addition to a constant and respectful behavior.
5. High standards are expected of each team member and must be understood by all team members.
6. The team must receive positive external feedback that is supportive and encouraging and that motivates each individual member as well as the team as a whole.
7. Team success must be based on ethical leadership. It is important that the team leader has high-quality leadership and communication skills. In addition to working for the benefit of the team he or she places needs of the team before individual members and is not interested in achieving personal goals or personal recognition or benefiting from the position.

SKILLS NEEDED FOR EFFECTIVE TEAM DEVELOPMENT

The instructor has the responsibility of developing and using strategies that encourage students to develop a productive team atmosphere. The following are examples of several effective factors:

- Student groups are divided into diverse groups so that they encounter students with divergent concerns, backgrounds, and interests.
- Design activities that promote awareness of diversity within the group and of the difficulties of working as a team.
- Engage students in activities that challenge them to develop trust in their teammates.
- Persuade students to participate willingly in discussions and asking questions.
- Encourage self-awareness that reflects on group work by having students fill out a check list regarding team environment and the process of learning and how they feel about the team. Converse with them on how to develop team unity and cohesiveness.

FACILITATING SMALL GROUPS

In a student-centered approach to learning students participate in small groups in class, and in some cases, out of class. Often, students do not have the knowledge and skills to work effectively in groups. However, if prompted, they are familiar with problems that can arise when working in groups, and they have some ideas about how to address these situations. Here are some of the questions that faculty members often ask about using small groups or teams as part of an approach to teaching.

The question often asked is: How should teams be formed? The instructor has the primary, but not the only, responsibility for creating a safe, productive learning environment. In general, the teams that are formed influence the learning environment that is created. As a result, the instructor has the responsibility for forming teams and it's important to see that teams get off to a good start?

Most instructors have students who do not have the knowledge or lack the ability to function effectively in a student team situation. Therefore, instructors must work to establish a learning environment that supports effective student team development. There are many challenges that occur when using student teams that must be effectively addressed at the beginning of the course. As groups are being formed, the facilitator can set the policies for addressing problems that may occur in the future.

How should teachers form the teams? The facilitator has the primary, but not the only, responsibility for creating a safe, productive learning environment. In general, the teams that are formed influence the learning environment that is created. The facilitator has a responsibility for forming effective teams.

How do I grade team assignments? Giving every team member the same grade on a single assignment submitted as a team does not promote individual accountability, one of the core elements of effective cooperative learning. Faculty members looking for alternatives should consider the following resources: Karl Smith offers the following suggestions to promote individual accountability: (1) keep group size small, (2) assign roles, (3) randomly ask one member of the group to explain what they're learning, (4) have students do work before the group meets, (5) have students use their group learning to do an individual task afterward, (6) everyone signs a participated agreement and can explain the information, and (7) observe and record individual contributions. (8) Establish peer assessment in which team members offer data to help discern and evaluate individual contributions; this is one approach to differentiating grades.

The Foundation Coalition also offers a resource on peer assessment and a resource on monitoring the progress of student teams on extended team assignments. For more in-depth information, teamwork skills and effective group members can be found on the Waterloo University website.

DECISION MAKING

Decision making that requires problem solving and critical thinking is a necessity for success in education and life. Problem solving is closely linked to creativity in assessing, identifying, and advancing the options useful in solving problems. In order for decision making to be effective, it must include the skills needed for creative development, option identification, clarity of judgment, firmness in decision making, and effective implementation if problems are to be solved. The following are procedures for making efficient decisions:

1. The decision maker must be clear when defining confronting issues.
2. Accumulate the facts necessary and their causes.
3. Brainstorm possible options and solutions.
4. Consider and evaluate all possible alternatives.
5. Make a decision on what is the most appropriate option.
6. Make certain all methods used were properly implemented.

Doing the right thing is the most important factor when making decisions. When comparing complex pros and cons, the most important factors in decision making are when the instructor and student are attempting to solve problems. What generally happens in complex problem solving situations is that there are a number of right answers. The key is to choose the best situation presented and make it work. The major problems confronting teachers and students in decision-making issues are comparing the pros (for) and cons (against).

PROBLEM SOLVING

The mark of an educated teacher and student is that he/she knows where to locate information. The most important products of an educational procedure are learning the skills in problem solving and that students must learn to explore, test, and communicate data that allow for logical rational decisions. Students learn and recall information more efficiently when they are challenged to seek answers to the unfamiliar and are motivated by curiosity to increase learning.

The first thing that instructors must decide on is the level of material which best fits the students' knowledge and intellectual ability. This will allow students to cultivate the ability to evaluate and recall previously studied material in order to refresh their memory and construct new knowledge. Educators should develop a learning atmosphere that contains several teaching methods. A cognitive learning situation must be one that includes directing awareness to the learning process itself which in turn will develop a self-learning problem-solving ability and environment.

Therefore, students should develop cognitive learning abilities by improving the ability to think, observe, experiment, and confirm their findings based on previous learning experiences. Having a process or strategy for solving problems helps to keep efforts focused and gets rid of delays.

Problem solving usually includes the following steps:

- Problem identification
- Analyze the problem and gather information
- Create potential solutions
- Choose and analyze the solution
- Analyze/evaluate the results

Some of the tools used in problem-solving include:

- Brainstorming: is used to encourage participation from each team member to produce new and creative ideas, while initiating a climate of freedom and openness, which encourages and increases the quantity of ideas.
- Divide and conquer: decrease the number of large and complex problems into smaller sections.
- Creative thinking: provides solutions indirectly and creatively.
- Evidence: a search for proof that the problem cannot be solved will provide a starting point.
- Root cause analysis: The objective of root cause analysis is to locate the primary cause of a problem.
- Cause and effect diagrams: These diagrams represent the association between an effect (the problem) and its probable causes. These diagrams help to sort out and relate the interactions among the factors present.

BRAINSTORMING

Alex F. Osborn in 1973, made popular the term brainstorming when he stated that that this process is more effective if students work together to generate ideas. There are several definitions for brainstorming. They consist of group techniques where efforts are made to find conclusions for specific problems. The following are techniques in the process of solving problems.

- Assessing information and by using problem solving, creative and critical thinking skills to construct new ideas
- A process by which all members of a group communicate ideas that solve problems
- Unusual ideas are proposed in which the end result combines them into a single idea
- Research must focus on quality research
- Criticism must be withheld
- Unusual ideas welcome

INDEPENDENT THINKING

The objective of independent thinking is to develop students who can think within themselves which must be the primary goal of every educator. Independent thinking is needed if students are to convince themselves that the information being researched or presented is accurate and logical. Independent thinking is different from the critical thinking in that critical thinking collects information to be studied in order to arrive at a logical conclusion.

Independent thinking, on the other hand, is the desire for students to think autonomously in reaching suppositions. Independent thinkers feel that it is intolerable to just reach a conclusion with what is being taught unless it is based on personal observation and experiences.

Although a difficult process, in swaying student thinking, there are procedures whereby the instructor can promote independent thinking. This can be accomplished by the facilitator asking difficult questions where thinking is required in place of simple recall.

This process now requires students to think on their own about the concept/s proposed by the instructor. Questioning the concepts and theories proposed by the instructor is another way to develop independent thinking. For this process to be successful, all students are involved in the brainstorming and problem-solving discussions.

Hunt (1971) proposed that if the environment is perfectly matched to the developmental level of learners; learners are more likely to remain at their current level of learning. Therefore, "students must learn to think on their own in order to realize a higher level of learning." In this type of active learning, students are more likely to be enthusiastically participating, mentally and/or physically, with their environment.

Clough's (1999) research suggested that even if students sit passively during a lecture, learning can occur if they are mentally active and selectively absorbing and attending to the information while connecting and comparing it to prior knowledge and any new information being presented.

CRITICAL THINKING

INTRODUCTION: Critical thinking is an important component of most professions and an important part of the education process and is increasingly important as students move through their secondary, university, or graduate education. However, there is dialogue among educators about its precise meaning and scope of critical thinking. The problem is that in critical thinking many students' thoughts are based on biased, imprecise lack of information and/or downright prejudice.

However, critical thinking has a great effect on the quality of a student's life, and what they make of themselves or build depends precisely on the quality of their thinking. Careless thinking is costly both in money and in quality of life. However, if students are to excel in life, their thoughts must be methodically promoted. For this reason the development of critical thinking-skills provides an important outlook on lifelong endeavors.

DEFINITIONS: Critical thinking is a tool by which the student or instructor can develop a reasoned conclusion that incorporates passion and creativity and is based and on guidance, discipline, and common sense. This process is an important and basic component of success in education and almost all areas of society.

Paul and Elder's (2008) definition of critical thinking as a method of thought about any topic, subject matter, or predicament takes place when students expand their quality judgment by skillfully taking control of the organization inherent in thinking and enforcing intellectual standards upon them. The following are the attributes of a well-educated critical thinker:

- To produce critical questions and problems, they must be expressed clearly and accurately.
- Accumulates and evaluates significant data by using conceptual ideas to interpret them effectively with well-reasoned conclusions and explanations.
- Communicates effectively with others in deciding how to solve complicated problems.
- Logical reflective thinking focused on deciding what to believe or do,
- The mental discipline to process actively while skillfully conceptualizing, applying, analyzing, synthesizing, or evaluating information gathered from, or generated by, observation, experience, reflection, reasoning, or communication, as a guide to belief and action.
- Self-regulatory decisive judgment, which result in interpretation, analysis, evaluation, and inference.
- Explanations based on judgments of evidential, conceptual, methodological, critical, or contextual considerations.
- Includes a commitment to using reason in the formulation of our beliefs.

Critical thinking generally requires the ability to recognize problems and to find workable solutions for solving those problems by assembling and organizing relevant information that recognizes unstated assumptions and values as well as to comprehend and use language with accuracy, clarity, and discrimination (Glaser 1941).

DEVELOPING CRITICAL THINKING SKILLS: The list of core critical-thinking skills includes observation, interpretation, analysis, inference, evaluation, explanation, and meta-cognition. The consensus among experts is that an individual or group engaged in strong critical thinking gives due consideration to establish evidence through observation and through context skills that provide relevant criteria for making sound judgment. There is a reasonable level of consensus among experts that for an individual or groups to engage in critical thinking, they should give consideration to establishing the following factors:

- Evidence through observation
- Context skills
- Relevant criteria for making a correct judgment
- Applying methods or techniques that form judgment
- Valid theoretical constructs for understanding the problem and the question at hand

In addition to possessing strong critical-thinking skills, students must be willing to engage in problem solving and making decisions using those skills. Critical thinking employs not only logic but broad intellectual criteria such as clarity, credibility, accuracy, precision, relevance, depth, breadth, significance, and fairness.

PROCEDURE: Critical thinking calls for the abilities to:

- Recognize the problems that occur in order to find workable means for solving problems
- Understanding the significance of prioritization in problem solving
- Collect and assemble relevant information
- Identify unstated assumptions and values
- Understand and use language with accuracy, clarity, and judgment
- Translate data to evaluate evidence and assess disagreements
- Recognize the existence (or nonexistence) of logical relationships concerning suggestions
- Describe reasonable conclusions and generalizations
- Assess the conclusions and generalizations at which the student gains recognitions
- Reform one's patterns of beliefs on the basis of wider knowledge
- Submit accurate judgments about specific things and qualities in everyday life

KEY IDEAS TO REMEMBER

A critical thinker puts forth persistent effort to examine any belief or supposed form of knowledge in the light of the evidence that supports it and the further conclusions which it cultivates. Irrespective of the sphere of thought, a well-cultivated critical thinker raises important questions and problems, formulating them clearly and precisely, while gathering and assessing relevant information. By using abstract ideas to interpret information, the student effectively comes to well-reasoned conclusions and solutions while testing them against relevant criteria and standards of thinking open-mindedly within alternative systems of thought. This requires students to recognize and assess, as need be, their assumptions, implications, and practical consequence.

References

ACTIVE LEARNING

Bonwell, C. C. and Edison, J. A. Active Learning (ASHEERIC).
e.How.com, Interactive Learning.
Felder, R. M. and Brent, R. *Learning by Doing*, Chem. Engr. Education (2003).
Felder, R. M. and Brent, R. *Active Learning* (North Carolina State University).
Hake, R. Interactive Engagement vs. Traditional Methods, *American Journal of Physics* (1998).
Higher Education Report, George Washington University (1991).
Johnson, D., Johnson, R. and Smith, K. *Active Learning in the College Classroom*, Edina, MN: Interaction Books (1998).
Prince, M. J. Does Active Learning Work? A Review of the Research. Engr. Education (2004)

COOPERATIVE LEARNING

Hertz-Lazarowitz, R. and Miller, N. (Eds.) *Interaction in Cooperative Groups: Theoretical Anatomy of Group Learning*, Cambridge: Cambridge University Press, (1992).
Johnson, D. and Johnson, R. *Cooperative and Competition Learning*, Edina, MN: Interactive Book Company (1989).
Johnson D. W. and Johnson, R. T. *Cooperation and Competition: Theory and Research*, Edina, MN: Interactive Book Company (1989).
Johnson, D. W. and Johnson, R. T. *Learning Together and Alone: Cooperative, Competitive and Individualistic Learning*, Englewood Cliffs, NJ: Prentice Hall (1991).
Johnson, D., Johnson, R. and Holubec, E. *Advanced Cooperative Learning*, Edina, MN: Interaction Book Company (1988).
Johnson, D., Johnson, R. and Smith K. What evidence is there that it works? *Chance* 30 (July/August 1998).
Kalgan, S. *The Structural Approach to Cooperative Learning*, Englewood Cliffs, NJ: Prentice-Hall (1990).
Sharan, Y. and Sharan, S. *Expanding Cooperative Learning through Group Investigation*, New York: Teachers College Press (1992).
Slavin, R. E., Research on cooperative learning and achievement: What we know that we need to know. *Contemporary Educational Psychology* 21 (1996): 43–69.
Tsay, M. and Brady, M., A case study of cooperative learning and communication (2010).

COLLABORATIVE LEARNING

Bruffee, K. *Collaborative Learning: Higher Education, Interdependence and the Authority of Knowledge*, Baltimore: Johns Hopkins University Press (1993).
Davis, B. G. Collaborative learning: Group work and study teams. In Barbara Gross Davis, *Tools for Teaching*, San Francisco: Jossey-Bass Publishers (1993).
Glaser, Edward, M. *An Experiment in the Development of Critical Thinking*, New York: Teacher's College, Columbia University (1941).
Goodsell, A. S., Maher, M. R. and Tinto, V., (Eds.). *Collaborative Learning: A Sourcebook for Higher Education*, National Center on Postsecondary Teaching, Learning and Assessment, Syracuse University Press (1992).
Prantiz, T., Collaborative Versus Cooperative: A Comparison of Two Concepts

CONSTRUCTIVISM LEARNING

Brooks, J. and Brooks, M., *In Search of Understanding: The Case for Constructivist Classrooms*, Association for Supervision and Curriculum (1993).
Duffy, T. M. and Johansson E., *Constructivism and the Technology of Instruction*, Hillsdale, NJ: Laurence Erlbaum (1992).
Glassfeld, E. *Cognition, Construction of Knowledge and Teaching.* Syntheses (1998).
Kolb, E. *Experimental Learning Experience as the Source of Learning and Development*, Englewood Cliffs, NJ: Prentice-Hall (1984). Meyer, D. L. The Poverty of Constructivism: Educational Philosophy and Theory (2009).

STUDENT-CENTERED LEARNING

Alexander, J. B. and McDaniel, G., Authentic assessment of problem-based learning: *Journal of Alabama Academy of Science* (2000).
Armstrong, J. Scott. Natural Learning in Higher Education, *ASHTERIXC Higher Education Report*, George Washington University (2012).
Australian Capital Territory Debating Union: Basic Debating Skills (2003).
Brown, Ann and Campione, Joseph C. Guided Discovery in a Community of Learners. (1994).
Dewey, John. Democracy and Education: An Introduction to the Philosophy of Learning.
DiMartino, Joseph and Clarke, John. Personalized Learning: Preparing High School Students to Create Their Futures, Lanham, MD: Rowman & Littlefield (2003).
Edens, M. E. Preparing Problem Solvers, College Teaching (2002).
Floyd Jeffery and Simpson. Student-Centered Learning (Texas A&M University).
Gardner, Howard. *The Disciplined Mind: What All Students Should Understand*, New York: Simon and Schuster (1999).
Goldfield R. C. Disorders of Reasoning and Problem-Solving Ability (1987).
Hills, H. *Team-Based Learning*, Burlington, VT: Gower (2001).
Mazur, E. *Peer Instruction: Getting Students to Think in Class*, Cambridge, MA: Harvard University (2003).
Meeks, Glenn. *Creating a Culture of Learning: Moving Towards Student Centered Learning*, Lanham, MD: Rowman & Littlefield (2014).
Richards, Paul. *Critical Thinking*, Englewood Cliffs, NJ: Prentice Hall (2006).
Savoie, J. M. and Workman, D. Problem-Based Learning Journal for Education of the Gift.
Williamson, Julie, *Literacy in the Student-Centered Classroom*, Lanham, MD: Rowman & Littlefield (2008).

About the Author

Professor Spooner's philosophy and objective of education is to train students to perform accurately, efficiently, and effectively in society. Therefore, the teacher's role becomes that of a facilitator who imparts information and knowledge that allows the student to achieve his or her goals. The facilitator develops a curriculum containing information and skills the students need to learn in order to achieve the desired results of instruction that are measured by various individual evaluation processes.

After graduating from San Diego State University in 1960 with a BA in social studies and in 1963 with an MA in education, an MA in history from Sonoma State University, and an MA in physical education from Wichita State University, Professor Spooner began his teaching career at the secondary level as a U.S. history, world history, and public speaking teacher and volleyball coach.

Upon graduation from Sonoma State University with an MA in U.S. history in 1988 and from Wichita State University with an MA in physical education in 1993, he began teaching history and speech at Galveston College and Texas A&M University in Galveston, Texas. In 1996, Professor Spooner accepted a position teaching U.S. history, public speaking, and lifetime wellness at Big Bend College in Washington. He continued to improve and upgrade his student-centered approach to learning with PowerPoint presentations and other media teaching methods. Due to student success and the appreciation of his teaching methods, he was chosen as a top ten instructor at Big Bend College on several occasions.

Professor/Coach Spooner is the author of two athletic books: 1) *The Science of Volleyball Practice and Drill Development*, which appeared on Amazon's best-sellers list and 2) *Catch the Magic: Athletics the Mental Game*.